CRIMES AND PUNISHMENT

VOLUME
22

Crimes and Punishment takes a hard and objective look at crime and criminals—their ways and methods and the means by which they are caught and punished. This authoritative edition combines material from *Murder Casebook, Science Against Crime,* and *Crimes and Punishment* which were originally published in the United Kingdom. This new compilation casts a penetrating eye upon the violence around us with which we must live.

CRIMES AND PUNISHMENT

The *Illustrated* CRIME ENCYCLOPEDIA

VOLUME
22

H. S. STUTTMAN, INC. *publishers*   Westport, CT 06889

CONTENTS

MURDER CASEBOOK Lucky Luciano
The story of the man who headed up Crime Inc and was overlord of its lethal arm, Murder Inc. The Outfit, the Mob, the Syndicate were all names for the organization he ran – the US Mafia.

Published by H. S. STUTTMAN INC.
Westport, Connecticut 06880
© H. S. STUTTMAN INC. 1994

Murder Casebook material
© Marshall Cavendish Limited 1989, 1990, 1991, 1994
Science Against Crime material
© Marshall Cavendish Limited 1982, 1994
Crimes and Punishment material
© Little Brown & Company 1973, 1974, 1975, 1976, 1994

TRIED BY HIS PEERS

Mabel Edith Scott was a beautiful young flower of the English aristocracy. But her mother, the widow of Sir Claude Scott, was a "venomous" and "avaricious" woman. She and her daughter were determined to milk Earl Russell of his fortune.

EARL RUSSELL, whose Prime Minister grandfather was treated as a friend by Queen Victoria, made the tragic mistake of choosing the wrong mother-in-law. Her evil and malicious scheming – and the way her false stories set society gossiping about his "depraved habits" – drove him to Reno in Nevada for the "divorce that never was". Eventually, after a sensational trial before his peers in the House of Lords, he was imprisoned for bigamy.

Friends had begged him not to be rushed into marrying the daughter of the widowed and venomous Lady Scott. The two women, they warned, were avaricious adventuresses. But Russell – who was orphaned as a small boy, and who was only 12 when he succeeded to the earldom on the death of his grandfather – was headstrong and independent. His maternal grandfather was the second Lord Stanley of Alderley, and Russell once said: "I am a Stanley in appearance and largely in temperament . . . blustering my way through life with the superb assurance and self-satisfaction of the true Stanley."

Drama

That was his assessment of himself, and he was confident that, at the age of 23, he was shrewd enough to pick the right mate.

Some of the stories circulating about Lady Scott, widow of Sir Claude Scott, were alarming. In Mayfair drawing-rooms it was whispered that some of her many admirers were not as respectable as might be wished. There was also the fact that, during their six months of courtship, 21-year-old Mabel Edith had been strangely volatile in her emotions – and, at times, overstrung to the point of hysteria. But she was exceptionally beautiful, and young Russell was sure that his steadying influence would mould her into a graceful and exemplary wife.

So, in February 1890, he stood before the high altar at the Church of St. Peter in London's select Eaton Square waiting for his bride. The cream of the British aristocracy was there, together with Ministers of State and senior army officers in their resplendent uniforms. This was an archetyped Establishment occasion, and the colourful scene inside the ornate church contrasted vividly with the dull and icy weather outside.

If Russell could have known how the ceremony was to plunge him into disgrace and tragedy – and cost him a veritable fortune – he might well have shocked the august congregation by fleeing from the church, leaving his bride standing at the altar.

Now it was too late. Mabel was at his side. And, as soon became horrifyingly obvious, the elegant and cosmopolitan Lady Scott was already congratulating herself. Russell, a man of enormous wealth and prestige, was ensnared – a captive of his own honourable vows.

"With my body I thee worship." Those words turned sour within the hour – for Mabel made it clear that she was not planning to do much worshipping, and drama erupted almost as soon as the "happy couple" left the church. Mabel, apparently as a back-lash against the tensions and excitement, collapsed in hysterics. Russell tried to comfort her, but was shushed away by Lady Scott, who hurried her daughter home and ordered her to bed.

Honeymoon cancelled

A doctor, who had been on friendly terms with Lady Scott for some time, immediately diagnosed pleurisy. As a result of this, Lady Scott insisted that the honeymoon at Torquay in Devon be cancelled. Russell – who later demanded that "common sense" should be introduced into Britain's divorce laws – spent his wedding night miserably alone in his home at Eaton Square.

After two weeks Lady Scott agreed that Mabel was fit enough to travel to Torquay. However, despite Russell's tenderness, there was still very little "worshipping". Within a few days of their arrival at the honeymoon hotel he found that his countess was very different from the girl who had been so anxious to marry him. She was wilful and spiteful and wildly extravagant. The quarrels which began on the honeymoon became more and more acrimonious after their return to London. Three months later, the unhappy marriage collapsed, and Mabel returned home to the welcoming arms of her mother.

Ultimatum

Society scandalmongers pounced upon this to enliven their tea-parties, and the Russell family – although it had never approved of the match – tried to engineer a reconciliation for the sake of their public image. It was now becoming obvious that Mabel, stage-managed by her mother, had seen one over-riding attraction in the young Earl Russell – the size of his cheque-book. Now she felt she had a claim to a large part of his money, and saw no reason to submit herself to any routine of respectable domesticity. But the Russells did win a reprieve, and Mabel was persuaded to return to the matrimonial home. It was, however, a brief reunion, for on June 12 – only five months after the wedding – Mabel left her husband for good.

She went to live with her mother at Bray Lodge near Maidenhead, in Berkshire, and gave Russell an ultimatum: he was to give her £1000 a year for life. In return she would undertake never to trouble him again. If only Russell had agreed – and he could easily have afforded the money – he would probably never have been condemned as a criminal, and thrown into prison.

Instead he said he would give her £80 a month on one condition only – that she should lead a "decently quiet life". Mabel, with the support of her mother, accepted the money but ignored the condition. Her extrovert behaviour with a rakish fast set infuriated Russell, and he gave instructions for the allowance to be stopped.

Soon after this, one of her cheques was returned by her bank marked "unpaid for lack of funds". This "insult and breach of faith" threw Lady Scott into a paroxysm of rage. Together with Mabel, she embarked upon a savage campaign of persecution.

Unfounded filth

At first the two women contented themselves with lawyers' letters which stated that Russell would be pressed to support his wife for life – even if he never saw her again. These were ignored by Russell. Mabel then took out papers for a judicial separation, but he remained unmoved. She threatened to start proceedings for divorce on the grounds of cruelty – and what would that do to his precious family honour? – but he still did not budge.

Then the venom really started to flow. If Russell did not do exactly what he was told, Mabel was going to prefer charges of homosexual misconduct between him and a young man who had stayed at the house before and after the wedding. Mabel claimed that she had absolute proof – although, in fact, her allegations were completely unfounded – and said she would publicly name the man concerned.

Lawyers advised Russell to give in. They were convinced that he would win any case, but they urged him to consider that many people would think "there is no smoke without fire". Also, for the sake of a mere £1000 a year, it was not worth dragging such an appalling and untrue story into public view. He disagreed. "The time," he said, "has come to fight."

So the battle moved into the courts. Russell, although he had expected unfounded filth to be thrown at him, was shocked at the extent of the allegations made by his wife and mother-in-law. They involved another man of unblemished reputation, and the mere reading of them in court could do Russell enormous harm. But he was determined that he must finally smash the tyranny of the two women. In December 1891 he stood solemnly in court to face the charge.

Mabel's evidence was so confused and thin that the lengthy proceedings degen-

erated into a shambles. The jury were not in the slightest bit surprised when the judge told them: "It is not true that the young man X was visited in his bedroom in the small hours of the night and morning on four separate occasions by Lord Russell. If it be not true, either Lady Russell has sworn to that she knows to be false, or she has sworn to that she does not know to be true . . . in either alternative, what is the value of her evidence upon any of the dozen or twenty subjects upon which she has spoken? The whole case against her husband rests upon her testimony, and if her testimony cannot be regarded as of any value in such a matter, what becomes of her case?"

Bizarre allegations

The jury acquitted Russell. Mabel was publicly denounced as a vicious liar – but she was not a woman to be stopped by such a minor detail. Within hours of leaving the court she was giving an interview to one of London's more notorious scandal-sheets. In it she insisted that she had not been allowed a fair hearing, and that the charges against her husband were totally true.

So the smears continued, and Russell, with immense dignity, tried to ignore them. In 1894 Mabel launched a new attack through her lawyers. Having repeatedly besmirched Russell's reputation with claims that she had written proof of his "unnatural" habits – coupled with regular demands for money from him – she now instituted proceedings for restitution of conjugal rights. She was anxious, apparently, to have this "homosexual monster" ordered back into her bed. Russell immediately replied by petitioning

for a judicial separation on the grounds of cruelty. He won.

Mabel and her mother brooded over their defeat, and then appealed against the verdict. The Appeal Court did give Mabel a partial victory – deciding that she had not been guilty of legal cruelty – at least not to such a degree as to constitute grounds for a judicial separation. However, her conduct had been infamous enough to stop them granting her appeal for restitution. This, Mabel felt, was a hollow victory. It brought her no money, and so she announced that she would carry her appeal to the House of Lords – and demand the restitution of her rights.

Russell entered a cross-appeal against the setting aside of his separation order – and that was the signal for a blizzard of foul and bizarre allegations from his mother-in-law. Every member of the House of Lords received letters claiming that unshakable proof of Russell's "sexual perversions" was in Lady Scott's possession. Similar letters were received by every member of the House of Commons, by lawyers, and by the most active gossipmongers in top Society.

Terrible indictment

To back up her slanders Lady Scott hired a small army of private detectives to winkle out any possible "evidence" against Russell. One was sent half-way round the world to find members of the crew who had sailed with Russell in his early yachting days as an Oxford under-

ON THE CRAGGY shores of Lake Tahoe, Nevada, Lord Russell and his true love Mollie settled down to await his divorce. But their "marriage" was illegal in Britain.

Radio Times Hulton

THE STEAM YACHT *ROYAL* was skippered by Lord Russell in his Oxford days. But according to vicious Lady Scott, his relationship with the crew was evil.

able. Russell had been steeped in tradition, and such an "unconventional procedure" seemed to have a tinge of salaciousness about it.

They discussed the possibilities with American friends, and were assured that, in some States, divorces—perfectly legal and respectable divorces—could be obtained virtually for the asking. So Russell sought the guidance of an attorney at Flagstaff, Arizona, who explained that domiciliary requirements varied from State to State—but that their best bet would be to go straight to Nevada. After living there for six months they could both be divorced and re-married again if they wished—all in a few minutes.

Bigamy

They moved to Nevada at the end of August and rented a small, unpretentious cottage on the shores of Lake Tahoe— where they settled down to wait out the six months. Then, in the spring of 1900, Russell divorced Mabel on the grounds of desertion and married Mollie. He cabled a triumphant announcement to *The Times* in London, and Mabel raged:

"My husband must have committed bigamy. I am in exactly the same position today as I was on my wedding day. I have never been served with any papers in connection with divorce proceedings in America. I know certainly that in America the divorce law is much more lax than it is in England, but he could not possibly have got a divorce from me without my knowing it. And he has no grounds for a suit against me, even for desertion.

"I am told that an Englishman can get naturalized in some parts of America in a very short while, and then he can marry legally if he has not been married in America before. My husband may have done this, and in that case I cannot take proceedings for bigamy against him over there. But if he comes to England . . . I don't know whether I should prosecute him then . . . I can scarcely think of it yet . . . I shall have to consult my lawyers . . ."

Ugly shock

The newly-weds returned to England almost immediately—although experts in English law warned them that the divorce and marriage might not be considered legally binding there. They were not concerned. They were married in their own eyes—and were not worried about whether or not they were technically living in sin.

However, there was still the problem of Mabel, and Russell determined to "buy her off" once and for all. She was only

graduate. Three young men were bullied and cajoled into signing a terrible indictment against their young skipper. If their statements were ever believed, Russell would unquestionably have been ruined. Lady Scott also bought "evidential" letters. One man, it was later discovered, had been promised £500 in cash and an income for life—if Lady Scott was successful in winning complete domination over the wealthy Russell.

There was only one course left open to Russell—he brought a charge of criminal libel against Lady Scott. The case was proved, and Mr. Justice Hawkins sentenced her to eight months' imprisonment. Even then she insisted on sticking to her preposterous story. Mabel, made of less tough material, had to be helped from the courtroom in screaming hysterics.

Dramatic role

Russell was never again to be troubled by his wife or his mother-in-law. Or so he thought. For a couple of years he submerged himself in an active political life; through his work he met the next woman who was to play such a dramatic role in

his story. Mollie Somerville certainly matched Mabel in beauty, and she was far more intelligent. She was a militant campaigner for women's rights, and, having heard her speak at a number of meetings, Russell became attracted to her.

Salaciousness

Mollie was already married for the second time—but she was not happy with her husband, and was in the process of divorcing him. She was flattered by the attention of such an eminent man as Russell (who was the elder brother of the philosopher Bertrand Russell). In 1899, frustrated by being legally fettered to Mabel, Russell suggested to his new love that they run away to start a completely fresh life, in June they left for America.

Very soon they were enchanted with their new country, and would gladly have forgotten all about England and its unhappy associations. There was, they heard, a possible option for them in what the English called "a double-quick American divorce". That might be the solution to their problem. But somehow it savoured of something not quite respect-

interested in money, and now that he had found such happiness, it was worth almost any price to see the last of her. A meeting was arranged, when it was agreed that Russell would ensure payment of £5000 to her if she sued him for divorce on the grounds of "technical bigamy". If she did not agree, he would ensure she did not receive a penny.

Mabel decided to take the money, and the English divorce went through. Russell was waiting until the end of the necessary six months for the decree to become absolute—so that he could marry Mollie again in England, thus making her a Countess—when he received an ugly shock. In June 1901 he was getting out of a train at London's Waterloo Station

when a Scotland Yard detective arrested him—and he was taken to Bow Street police court on a charge of bigamy.

So, after all that time back in England—when he had never made any secret of his activities in America—someone had decided to bring a charge. Who? Mabel? Russell's mother-in-law? He never found the answer, but he insisted

that the unknown person was clearly motivated by malice.

After a preliminary hearing at Bow Street, Russell was remanded to the Old

A BROKEN ARISTOCRAT stands before his peers. On July 18, 1901, Lord Russell heard the Lord High Steward read his sentence: three months in a common jail.

Bailey and convicted of felony. The criminal courts could convict a peer, but at that time they did not have the power to punish him—so the proceedings had to be transferred to the House of Lords.

This was desperately unfortunate for Russell. Informed public opinion was that in an ordinary court he would have been given no more than a nominal one day

in prison—which would have meant his immediate release. But an elaborate state trial in the Royal Gallery at Westminster —that could be a very different matter. The Lords would be so jealous of their reputation for impartiality—so keen to prove they were not giving preferential treatment to one of their own rank—that they might be far more severe.

Mansell Collection

The hearing was called for July 18, 1901, and the Lord Chancellor, Lord Halsbury, was appointed Lord High Steward. The Attorney General and the Solicitor General acted for the Crown. Russell was asked how he intended to plead, but before he could reply his lawyer rose to address the House on a point of law. Did the House have any right to try Lord Russell? A man owed temporary allegiance to the laws of the country in which he was domiciled. If he broke those laws he was punished by that country. Lord Russell, when living in Nevada, had in no way offended against the laws of that State—for his divorce and marriage there were both in accord with the laws of the land. Surely no English court, not even the House of Lords, was competent to judge a man over events which had taken place in America, and were perfectly legal there.

Pleading guilty

Many people present considered this extremely reasonable, but Lord Halsbury dismissed it. The case, he said, was too plain for argument. So Russell, after a lengthy discussion with his lawyer, reluctantly entered a plea of "guilty".

Russell, knuckles bunched tight, stood to address the House on his own behalf: "My Lords, it is . . . with the utmost reluctance and distaste that I have pleaded guilty to this indictment, but I have done so on the advice of my Counsel. And in saying that, My Lords, I do not wish it to be supposed that I reflect for one moment upon my Counsel or upon their advice—for more devoted, more painstaking and more loyal advisers than I have had in this case no unfortunate prisoner could wish.

"My Lords, I find myself here pleading guilty to this indictment within one month only of my apprehension upon this charge of bigamy. I am told, and I must accept it as a fact, that I was mistaken in supposing that I had a defence to the charge. I thought, My Lords, that I had acquired a proper domicile in Nevada—a sufficient domicile. I believed, My Lords, in the goodness of that decree in Nevada, and in the righteousness of my marriage there.

A mistake

"My Lords, I spent in Nevada something like eight months, for the purpose of obtaining that decree, and for the purpose of obtaining that residence which gives one a domicile according to American law. I should not have spent so long there if I had not supposed that the result of the proceedings would give me a valid opportunity of giving a social and legal sanction to my new home.

"I am told, My Lords, that I am mistaken, and I am told so now for the first time. . . but when I was in America and when I first came back to this country, neither then nor for some time after my return in this country did I suppose for one moment that I was breaking the criminal law of this country. My Lords, I would not have broken the laws of the country willingly or defiantly. Your Lordships are not to suppose that it was in any spirit of bravado or in any spirit of defiance that I endeavoured to set myself above the laws of my own country.

"I did not know, and I venture to say that 99 laymen out of 100 would not know, that under any circumstances a second marriage in a foreign State could be punishable as bigamy in this country. Still less, My Lords, did I think that a second marriage which was valid and at this day undisputed in the State of Nevada could be the subject of prosecution for bigamy here.

"My Lords, I am advised I have made a mistake, and I have therefore pleaded Guilty, and I am now, My Lords, only awaiting until the dissolution according to English law of my previous marriage has taken place, to marry again, according to the laws of this country, the lady with whom I went through the ceremony of marriage in Nevada. My Lords, I shall then have satisfied the laws of my own country as well as the laws of Nevada. I shall then have contracted legally that union which I have now contracted not only illegally, but, I am told, criminally . . . I can only leave myself to the judgment of Your Lordships and ask for what indulgence Your Lordships may see fit to give me."

Eternity

After the peers had deliberated for some 15 minutes, Lord Halsbury pronounced the sentence: "John Francis Stanley, Earl Russell, you have been convicted upon your own confession of felony. I need not say how painful it is to all Their Lordships that a great historic name should be degraded by such a conviction. At the same time . . . Their Lordships have unanimously arrived at the conclusion that justice will be satisfied in this case by your being imprisoned in Holloway for three calendar months, and as a criminal of the first division. That is the sentence."

Being bundled into the common jail was a nightmare experience for the fastidious Russell. He was allowed to receive just three letters a week, in addition to three visits—all of which were made by Mollie. It seemed, he said, "an eternity" until his release and his return to his "wife". But their ending was to be a sad one.

Fourteen years passed, then, in July 1915, Mollie Countess Russell petitioned for divorce on the grounds of her husband's statutory desertion and miscon-

WINSOME Mabel (left), despite her pose she was a wilful and quarrelsome woman. Above, Lord Russell, head held high, walks off to serve out his sentence.

duct. In court a letter she had written to him was read:

"Dear Frank, I still think you can't be serious in this assertion of yours that you are determined to break up our married life which has lasted nearly fourteen years. I really look upon your action in leaving as a form of self-denial, for you left on Ash Wednesday, the beginning of Lent. You see I cannot take you seriously, and I hope on receipt of this you will return to your home and wife, who will be prepared to welcome you and forgive the past—yours affectionately, Mollie Russell."

Third wife

His written reply said: "I can only tell you again that I am, after long consideration, firmly and finally resolved not to continue living with you. I have no quarrel with you and bear you no ill-will, but it would be impossible."

The following year—after having been awarded a free pardon for his previous crime—he married his third wife, Baroness von Arnim, the novelist. He later wrote "My Life and Adventures", and became Parliamentary Secretary to the Ministry of Transport towards the end of his life.

THE LUST OF FILTHY LUCRE

Lord William Russell lay dead, his throat slashed with a kitchen carving knife. In the dock, on trial for the murder, was his 23-year-old butler François Benjamin Courvoisier, a young man of impeccable references and demeanour. The evidence against him was purely circumstantial and somewhat flimsy, yet who else could have gained access so easily to his master . . . ?

FOR six weeks his name had been on everybody's lips, below stairs as well as above, in fashionable London clubs and the echoing corridors of the House of Commons. Now, at last, the truth would be known. Had François Benjamin Courvoisier, 23-year-old Swiss butler-valet, cut the throat of his master, 73-year-old Lord William Russell, with a carving knife? Or, as Courvoisier had been at pains to suggest, was the gruesome crime carried out as Lord William slept in his bed, the work of a burglar?

The case—and the trial that was about to begin—has aroused so much interest that even some newspaper reporters were excluded from the courtroom to allow more space for members of society and the nobility. Sir Nicholas Tindale, the presiding judge, and Mr. Baron Parke, his associate, were so hemmed in by elegantly gowned ladies on the bench that they scarcely had room to move.

Missing items

They leaned forward as Courvoisier took his place in the dock. He wore a black suit which accentuated the pallor of his face and the straw colour of his hair. He made a dignified and ceremonious bow to the court, then stood erect while the charge against him was read. At the end he paused before replying, in a firm and suave voice: "Not guilty."

The housemaid, Sarah Mancer, had found Lord William dead in his bed on the morning of May 6, 1840. He lay on a pillow soaked with blood. The murderer had taken the unusual step of covering his victim's face with a towel, also stained with blood when the body was found. The house—at 14 Norfolk Street—appeared to have been ransacked, and an inventory disclosed that a number of items were actually missing. They included whatever money Lord William might have had in his possession, five rings, a pair of cufflinks, a Waterloo medal, Lord William's fob-watch, and 14 silver spoons and forks, all engraved with the family crest, a goat.

It was known that, a couple of days before his death, Lord William had drawn £20 from his bank in the form of one £10 note, one £5 note, and five sovereigns. A £5 note and six sovereigns had been found in a purse in a box belonging to Courvoisier. A mark showed that the £5 note had come from Lord William's bank, but Courvoisier explained the fact that it was in his possession by saying: "I gave Lord William five sovereigns' change for it."

By the time of Courvoisier's arrest, two days after the murder, a thorough search of the house had uncovered the greater part of the missing items, hidden in odd crevices. No evidence had been found, however, that it was Courvoisier who had concealed them, and there was no trace at all of the silver spoons and forks.

VICTIM—but why? Lord Russell was undoubtedly a wealthy man by any standards, yet the killer had stolen so little that the whole act seemed useless.

That, plus the fact that the house had apparently been broken into by an intruder, was the strongest factor in Courvoisier's favour. When the housemaid ran downstairs to fetch help at 6 a.m., after finding Lord William's body, she discovered the bolts of the front door drawn and the chain off. Inspector John Tedman, one of the police officers called to the scene, had also reported that Courvoisier said to him: "We have been robbed. Here's where they came in"—and led him to the door into the backyard, where he pointed out scratches on the woodwork and the top bolt hanging loose.

The apparent break-in—a fake, in his view—was one of the early points raised by prosecutor Mr. John Adolphus in his opening address. "It will be shown," he said, "that the marks on the back door and its post were made from within the house, not from outside. The front door, locked and bolted soon after 10 p.m., was found unlocked and unbolted next morning. The way various articles were strewn about on the floor by the door suggests an attempt to create the impression that a burglar had entered from the back, taken alarm and gone out by the front door."

Some of the missing articles, he also pointed out, had been found in a place to which Courvoisier had special access—his pantry. "From almost the moment the murder was discovered, the house was in the possession of the police," said Mr. Adolphus. "Courvoisier was kept separated from the other two servants—Sarah Mancer and the cook, Mary Hannel—and was under constant police supervision. It is impossible that any person other than the prisoner could have hidden those articles."

White gloves, a handkerchief, and a "dickey" shirt front spattered with blood spots had been found in Courvoisier's box. Mr. Adolphus did not make much of that. The items had been discovered the second, not the first, time the box was searched. He was anxious to forestall what he knew would be the defence line—that the police had planted the items in the hope of collecting the £400 reward offered by the Russell family for the unmasking of the killer.

Unusual statement

Instead, he returned to the missing items which had turned up in the butler's pantry. They consisted of a £10 note, known—like the £5 note discovered in the prisoner's box—to have been in Lord William's possession earlier, three sovereigns, a Waterloo medal, the fob-watch and the rings. "Had a thief *entered*," said Mr. Adolphus, "he would have taken these things away. But observe the fact that they were found in the place to which the valet had peculiar access."

He ended the prosecution address with an unusual statement. "The prisoner," he said, "is a foreigner. Foreigners believe that English noblemen carry vast sums of gold about with them. With foreigners, murder is only too common a prelude to robbery, for they imagine that, if they destroy the life of the person they rob, there will exist no testimony against them." This argument from the general to the particular caused many raised eyebrows in legal circles, and gave the defence what has been described by one expert as "a fine topic" when it came to their turn to address the jury.

Brilliant lawyer

Sarah Mancer and Mary Hannel were the first two witnesses. With their help the prosecution began to build its case, strong on circumstantial evidence, low on direct. There was also the suggestion of a motive. Lord William had been showing annoyance about the carelessness of Courvoisier, who had been in his service only five weeks. Only the afternoon before the murder he had given Courvoisier a bawling out for not delivering a letter to Brooks's Club on time.

That same night Courvoisier had volunteered—for the first time since joining the household—to go out and get some beer for the cook and housemaid. "After drinking only a small glass, I felt very

drowsy," said Sarah Mancer. "Next morning I had considerable difficulty in arousing the cook, who had drunk far more than I had." She agreed that "something must have been put in the beer." Said Mary Hannel: "I felt very tired after drinking the beer. When I went to bed I fell asleep at once."

This first day of the trial—Thursday, June 18—was to end disastrously for the prosecution, however. Constable Baldwin, one of the first policemen at the house, was the last witness of the day, and, in the words of one celebrated author, Mr. Charles Phillips, the brilliant lawyer defending Courvoisier, "fell upon Baldwin and tossed and gored him".

HIS LORDSHIP'S HOUSE was situated in London's elegant Park Lane. There were easier ways to get in than by breaking the locks on the back door . . .

At the inquest, held 24 hours after Lord William's death, Baldwin had said the backyard door of the house appeared to have been forced from the outside. Now he said the forcing appeared to have been faked from the inside. Mr. Phillips was on to him instantly.

Mr. Phillips: Have you heard of £400 for information which leads to the arrest and conviction of the murderer?

Baldwin: No.

Mr. Phillips: Have you not seen the

de Clifford. "Lady de Clifford handed it to Lord William to pass on to his sister-in-law, Lady Janet Bailey, to be used for charity," he explained.

While the prosecution case rested on circumstantial evidence, the defence relied almost entirely on character witnesses. Lady Julia Lockwood, for whom the prisoner had served as a second footman for nine months, considered him "quiet, harmless and inoffensive".

"I never had any reason to suspect him of dishonesty," she said. An M.P. named Fector, in whose household the prisoner had worked for two years, described him as "obliging, efficient and respectful, was on good terms with everyone," he stated.

Kindness

Peter Jellings, owner of the Hotel Bristol in Jermyn Street, said: "The prisoner worked for me as a waiter from about the time he arrived in England four years ago until he entered private service. He worked hard and was well-liked. I was impressed with his kindness and the humanity of his disposition."

The feeling throughout London at the end of the day was that there was enough evidence to convict Courvoisier of theft, but not of murder. The missing silver suggested at least an accomplice. While there was the possibility of a second person involved, who might have been the killer, it was unlikely that any jury would convict.

Mr. Adolphus was not in court to hear the last of the character evidence. As Counsel for the Crown, he had been summoned to a conference with the Attorney-General over a High Treason charge against a mulatto named Edward Oxford. Nine days earlier, Oxford had tried to shoot Queen Victoria as she drove with Prince Albert, her consort of four months, in a carriage up Constitution Hill.

Small parcel

Meantime, while Mr. Adolphus discussed the High Treason case and Courvoisier relaxed in the dock, listening to the glowing tributes to his character, a man named Joseph Vincent sat in the Hotel Dieppe, a dingy flophouse for commercial travellers off Leicester Square, reading a French-language newspaper. The newspaper was some days old, but it contained news of Courvoisier's forthcoming trial, gave details of the missing silver, and suggested the police might, if they had not already done so, concentrate their search "on known resorts of foreigners in London, such as Soho".

Joseph Vincent was co-proprietor of

bills advertising the reward?

Baldwin: I am too busy a man to stop and read public notices.

Mr. Phillips: The information about the reward was read aloud in General Orders to all police officers. Did you not hear it?

Baldwin: No.

Mr. Phillips pursued his line of questioning, and Baldwin eventually, but clearly reluctantly, was forced to admit that he had read bills advertising the reward, had heard about the reward in General Orders, and would consider £400 a great deal of money. The implication was strong and clear: Courvoisier was being framed for the reward money.

Extensive search

In the clubs and salons of Mayfair that night, betting was heavily in favour of Courvoisier going free. Not only had Mr. Phillips scored heavily for the defence. Where were the silver spoons and forks, bulkiest of all the missing items? Police had been unable to find them in the house. Yet Courvoisier had been under police supervision from the time the murder was discovered until his arrest. He had not left the house. Therefore, whoever had made off with the spoons and forks could well be the killer.

This was one of the points Mr. Phillips concentrated on when he cross-examined

Inspector Tedman, the second police witness, next day.

Mr. Phillips: I am given to understand that several articles of table silver are alleged to be missing.

Tedman: Yes, sir, 14 table forks and spoons. They were included on the inventory, which was checked and signed by the prisoner when he took charge from the former valet.

Mr. Phillips: You made an extensive search of the whole premises, had the carpets up, the drains up, and sweeps to search every chimney—from attic to basement the search was made?

Tedman: Yes, sir.

Mr. Phillips: The prisoner did not leave the premises after ten o'clock on the night before the crime; he was segregated from the other servants and not permitted to hold any communication with anyone from outside the premises—yet no piece of those missing forks and spoons has been found?

Tedman: No, sir.

Mr. Phillips: Nor heard of?

Tedman: No, sir.

One of the last defence witnesses was Thomas Wing, the Russell family solicitor. He identified the £10 note found hidden in Courvoisier's pantry by initials on its back. It was one he had drawn in a cheque for £200 on behalf of another client, Lady

the hotel with a Frenchman named Louis Piolaine, who had married Vincent's cousin, Charlotte. With Piolaine absent abroad, he decided to show the newspaper to Charlotte, to make sure everything was in order if the police did carry out a search at this late date — and his action ensured that Courvoisier went to the gallows.

The name Courvoisier meant nothing to Charlotte. "But do you remember a young Swiss fellow named Jean who worked for us for a few weeks four years ago?" she said. "He had just come to this country from Geneva. Courvoisier is supposed to have come here at that time as well. They are about the same age. Perhaps they are the same person and Jean gave us a false name."

What had really made her suspicious, however, was that Jean had suddenly reappeared on a Sunday evening six weeks earlier — about the time of the murder — and given her a small parcel to care for until he returned for it. She went to a cupboard and took it out. It was wrapped in good-quality brown paper, every knot had been carefully sealed, and the parcel seemed unusually heavy for its size. "What should we do?" she asked.

They decided eventually to consult a solicitor they knew, Mr. Richard Cumming. The parcel was opened in his presence. Inside were the missing spoons and forks with the Russell crest.

The police, angry at the savaging they had already experienced at the hands of defence counsel, worked all night to line up witnesses to prove this new piece of evidence. The next morning Madame Piolaine was taken to Newgate Prison. From a window overlooking the exercise yard she identified Courvoisier as the "Jean" who had left the parcel containing

ELEGANT lords and ladies graced the trial, even squeezing out some news reporters. A few misguidedly decided to champion the cause of the accused man!

the silver with her.

News of the identification was given to Courvoisier almost at once. He paled as he realized the significance — the possibility of an intruder or an accomplice who had actually cut Lord William's throat had now been destroyed — and, as soon as he reached court, he asked to see Mr. Phillips. "They have found the silver," he said. "I gave it to a Madame Piolaine in a parcel to look after for me. I have admitted it."

This is believed to be the only time in British legal history that a piece of conclusive evidence has been produced on the last day of a murder trial. In the circum-stances it is hardly surprising that, with his fickle temperament, Mr. Phillips re-acted in a way that did serious damage to his career and was to haunt him to the end of his days at the bar.

Embarrassing position

He sought an interview with Mr. Baron Parke, the associate judge, and told him what had happened. This placed Mr Parke, who was trying the case just as much as the presiding judge was, in an extremely embarrassing position. It was also a serious breach of legal etiquette — as any statement by a prisoner to his solicitor or counsel should be sacred. Mr. Parke advised Mr. Phillips to do the best he could to defend his client on the evidence available.

Sweat poured from Courvoisier's brow and he nearly fainted as Madame Piolaine entered the witness box and described how he had brought the parcel to her on the Sunday before the murder. "He said he would call for it on the Tuesday following [the night of the killing]," she said. "I put the parcel in a cupboard and locked it up. He did not call for it on the Tuesday following and I never saw him again until today."

The supporting testimony included damaging evidence from an art dealer

FIRING at the Queen . . . A contemporary representation of the attempt by Edward Oxford to assassinate Queen Victoria.

named Moreno. "About nine days before his death, Lord William bought a print of *The Vision of Ezekiel* from me," he told the court. "The paper used for the parcel is the very piece in which I wrapped the print. It has my label stuck on it."

Mr. Phillips was not in his usual sparkling form when he rose to speak against the formidable array of circumstantial evidence that had been marshalled against the prisoner. He began by attacking the Crown's attempt to excite prejudice by telling the jury that "it was the common practice of foreigners to murder where they robbed". "Murder is a rare crime in Switzerland," he said, "and the Swiss are known for their virtuous character."

Forlorn task

The prisoner, he claimed, had no motive of hatred, jealousy or revenge. "Who put the bloodstained gloves and shirt front into the prisoner's box?" he asked. "I assert freely and fearlessly that they were placed there by some of the police. Baldwin, you will recall, lied on his oath." And, he pointed out, was it not odd that, despite the most stringent tests, in which Courvoisier had co-operated fully, not a spot of blood, nor a scratch, had been discovered on his clothes or person?

As for Madame Piolaine's evidence, he said: "If this be true, it is conclusive not of murder, but of robbery. If the prisoner is acquitted of the charge, he will still be answerable for the robbery."

Mr. Phillips spoke for three hours, but

against the evidence, and the presiding judge's summing-up, he had by now a forlorn task. Some of the telling points against the prisoner made by Sir Nicholas Tindale were: "If it was a genuine robbery, the thief did not pursue the ordinary course. Instead of getting into the house by the glass-panelled door at the back of the dining-room, which afforded easy access, he appears to have broken open the door into the lower area—and broken open that door with some violence. Moreover, if thieves entered for the purpose of plunder, would they have left behind them so many articles of value which they might have disposed about their persons . . .

". . . Many of the articles concealed in the pantry had been kept by the deceased in drawers in his bedroom. How far was a stranger likely to know where to find them, or to choose such a place in which to conceal them? . . ."

Confessions

It took the jury only 85 minutes to find Courvoisier guilty. In sentencing him to hang on Monday, July 6, Sir Nicholas said: "What may have been your precise and actual motive it is impossible to state. I fear it was the lust of filthy lucre." Courvoisier heard the verdict, the judge's words, and the sentence with no outward sign of emotion.

Within 48 hours Courvoisier had written the first of three confessions he was to make. He blamed envy and an inflammatory book he had read for a decision

to rob Lord William. He had killed when his master caught him in the act of robbery. It seems to have been his intention to rally support for his sympathizers—some of them prominent people—in the hope of getting his sentence commuted to life imprisonment.

When that failed, he tried to appeal to the Christian spirit of the age by claiming that a combination of drink and the works of Satan had led him to murder. That got him nowhere either. His third confession, written a few hours before he went to the scaffold, admitted that robbery and a desire for the easy life had been behind the murder. "I went into the dining-room and took a knife from the sideboard," he wrote. "I then went upstairs. I opened the bedroom door and heard him snoring in his sleep. There was a rushlight in the room at the time. I went near the bed, by the window side, and then I murdered him. He just moved his arm a little and never spoke a word."

In each confession Courvoisier explained the mysterious fact that no blood had been found on his clothing by saying: "I turned back the right sleeves of my shirt and jacket." Seconds before they hanged him, however, he confessed to one of the officials present: "I actually committed the crime in the nude. Afterwards I had only to wash myself at the sink."

THE TEACHER WHO DIED FOR LOVE

"Make love, not war," said the bumper sticker on her little red Citroen. But when Gabrielle Russier tried to practise what she preached, she and her 16-year-old pupil-lover (left) were crushed by the full force of pitiless morality and law . . . until she paid for her passion with her life.

John Hillelson

NOBODY could have called Gabrielle Russier beautiful, least of all sexually provocative. She was five feet tall, weighed less than 90 pounds and had a sheep-like face with a prominent nose and close-cropped hair. Although she was 31, she looked more like a youth of 18.

She was a familiar figure in the streets of Marseilles, driving her blood-red Citroen *Dyane* emblazoned with the slogan, "Make Love, Not War". And it was because she made love, not war, that the weight of the French legal system crashed down on her, crushing her to death.

France is popularly regarded as a land of lovers. Indeed, a tolerant and understanding eye is usually turned to the kind of illicit affair that would raise the same eyebrow in other countries.

However, Gabrielle Russier broke the forbidden rule. She boasted of her love, flaunted it, defied what she considered to be the bourgeois attitudes of society. Unfortunately for her, the attitudes she despised formed the very foundation of the French way of life.

It was alarming enough to conventional morality that Gabrielle's lover was a 16-year-old boy. What made it intolerable was that he was her classroom pupil and she was his teacher.

A terrible price

The love of an older woman for an adolescent boy is a stock element of French literature. It forms the basis of countless plays and novels—such as Colette's *The Ripening Seed*. The ultimate tragedy of bookish, academic Gabrielle Russier was that she confused the heady passions of literature with the hard-headed practicalities of real life. For her unworldliness, she paid a terrible price.

Not that her lover, Christian Rossi, was a shy and timid youth, led astray by a woman twice his age. Although only 16, he was tall for his years, heavily bearded, mature and confident. His political attitudes were extreme leftist, and he had already become a veteran of student demonstrations.

If frail and birdlike Gabrielle Russier didn't resemble a 31-year-old divorced mother of two, nor did Christian Rossi look like a 16-year-old schoolboy. The law, however, saw things differently. As far as they were concerned, Christian was a minor and Gabrielle Russier had abused her position of trust to seduce and "corrupt" him. But, in a way which the authorities could never understand, all Gabrielle's pupils at the Lycée Saint-Exupéry in Marseilles loved her. For she was one of them.

BEARDED, mature and confident, Christian Rossi wasn't exactly "seduced" by his older mistress. Ironically, it was her naïveté that undid them.

French teaching methods were old fashioned and autocratic. The teachers tended to be remote and unapproachable; an informal teacher-pupil relationship was virtually unknown. But Gabrielle broke the reactionary rules. Her pupils nicknamed her *Gatito*—"The Little Cat"—and addressed her with the familiar *tu*. In the evenings, she invited them to her flat to work, talk, and listen to records. More important, she was on their side politically. Her views were fashionably left-wing, and she was regarded as an ally in the unending student battle against authority and entrenched ideas.

Despite his years, Christian Rossi was one of Gabrielle's most politically active pupils. Both his parents were university professors and Communists—although his own ideas stemmed from Peking and the teachings of Mao Tse-tung. Appropriately, the events that brought Gabrielle and Christian together outside the classroom were the student riots of May, 1968, when young people in France erupted in a frenzy of politically inspired passion.

The prevailing mood—apart from the anger directed at established authority—was hope and idealism. In this hothouse climate, their love flourished. Christian initiated Gabrielle into the mystique of his particular brand of committed politics. In turn, she drew closer to him, and it was Gabrielle who suggested their first "date".

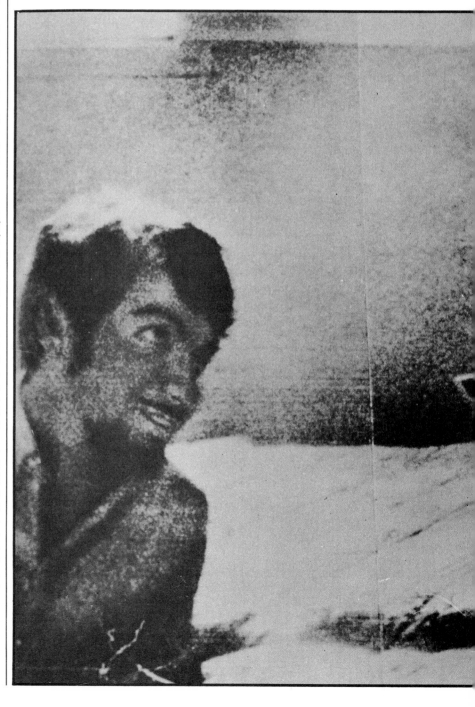

She invited Christian to the movies, but he would only agree if she attended a Maoist meeting with him first, and also obtained permission from his parents. Absurdly for a woman of 31, Gabrielle telephoned the Rossis and obtained their consent. The Rossis could have had no idea what they were starting.

Out the train window

Five weeks later — dispensing with the formality of ringing the Rossis — Gabrielle and Christian went on holiday together to Italy. On the principle that two's company and three's a crowd, Gabrielle got rid of the boy who was supposed to be travelling with Christian by the simple but effective method of throwing his suitcases from the train window.

Still unaware of the relationship, the Rossis sent Christian to stay with a German family for the summer. He had only been there a few days when Gabrielle turned up in her "Make Love, Not War" car and, posing as his cousin, drove him back to her apartment in Marseilles. So far, their affair had been secret and clandestine. Now Gabrielle made the mistake of bringing it into the open. She confronted M. Rossi and asked for his permission to let Christian live with her.

M. Rossi was appalled. "Leave my boy alone!" he shouted at Gabrielle, who fled sobbing from the room.

At first, the Rossis thought Christian was merely infatuated. They told friends that he was "bewitched" and "under a spell". But as the true situation dawned on them — exacerbated by continual arguments and Christian's frequent disappearances from home — their attitude hardened.

Thwarted by the Rossis in her desire for Christian, Gabrielle suffered a nervous breakdown. She trembled uncontrollably and was unable to speak above a whisper. Her work suffered, and in October, 1968, she went on sick leave. While Gabrielle was away from her school, the Rossis took what seemed to them the obvious step and packed Christian off to a boarding school in the Pyrenees. Equally predictably, Gabrielle followed him. After one secret visit, they were discovered kissing in her car and marched off to the local police station.

Rumours of the affair had already reached the Ministry of Education, who made a brave attempt to cool Gabrielle's ardour. They offered her a position hundreds of miles away at the University of Rennes. Although it was a big step upwards for Gabrielle — a brilliant scholar with an advanced university degree — she turned it down.

The instant Christian heard of the offer, he packed a handful of belongings and ran away from his new school. In Marseilles, Gabrielle hid him with friends . . . and in doing so gave the Rossis the opportunity they had been waiting for. For Gabrielle had unwittingly broken the law.

Corruption of minors

In France, anyone who "by fraud or violence" removes a minor "from the place where he had been put by those in authority over him" risks a maximum of 10 years in jail. The law is called *Détournement de Mineur,* and although it also implies corruption of minors, it specifically covers the offence of causing a child to leave home. While everybody else was still trying to handle the affair as discreetly as possible, the Rossis took the one step no one had foreseen. Invoking the law of *Détournement de Mineur,* they brought Gabrielle to court.

At first, Gabrielle was referred to as "X", but within a few days her identity had leaked out. Even at this stage, if she had been humble and contrite, the whole affair might have been quietly slipped into the legal filing-cabinet. But no. She committed the second unforgivable sin — actionable in French law — of answering back the Examining Magistrate. When he asked where Christian was hiding, she answered, "Find out for yourself, it's your job." The Magistrate warned her of the consequences, and she retorted, "All right, then, arrest me."

The police took her at her word. Only three weeks after Christian disappeared, four officers led by a magistrate raided

Gamma

Gabrielle's apartment. While she was being charged and formally arrested, they turned the place upside down. Disgruntled at not finding Christian, they combed the apartment for four hours, searching for any evidence on which further charges could be pinned. They examined her bathroom for signs of orgies, sifted kitchen herbs in the hope of finding drugs.

At the police station, Gabrielle had to undergo the humiliation of being stripped naked and searched in front of other prisoners. Although charged with only a minor offence — and far from being convicted — she was placed in "preventive detention". For the first time, there was public uproar on her behalf.

Legal commentators described it as a scandal that a person of Gabrielle's background and education should be refused bail. Popular newspapers presented her as a tragic figure, torn by love and duty. Left-wing political reviews — one-fifth of the French electorate regularly votes Communist — inveighed against the Rossis for betraying their principles — but Gabrielle stayed in jail.

Delinquent adolescents

It was clear that the authorities intended to keep Gabrielle behind bars until Christian gave himself up. The boy had no alternative. He came out of hiding — only to be immediately committed by a judge, at his parents' request, to a home for delinquent adolescents.

After Christmas, 1968, he was transferred to a private psychiatric clinic, where he was put on tranquillizers. It was a living death. There was nobody to talk to, nothing to keep him occupied. One day, he escaped and fled back to Gabrielle's apartment — to which she had now been returned. When she opened the door and saw his gaunt and wild-eyed figure, she burst into tears. But the Rossis weren't going to be blocked so easily. Convinced they were doing the "right thing", they snatched up Christian once more and sent him back to the home for delinquents. From there, he was shuttled to a boys' home. If the Rossis thought that by keeping Christian on the move they could steer him away from Gabrielle, then they were sadly mistaken. Every weekend Christian left the home and stayed at Gabrielle's flat.

However, both the law and the Rossis were losing patience. Gabrielle and Christian were summoned to the Palace of Justice for an official warning. But only one was set free. As he was walking down the steps of the Palace, Christian was suddenly seized by two men who dragged him to a waiting ambulance. Acting on his parents' instructions, they drove him back to the psychiatric clinic from which he had escaped a few months earlier.

This time, he was locked in a padded

Both Domenech

PRISON LIFE was a shattering experience for cultured Gabrielle (far left, with lawyer). Cellmates in Les Baumettes jail (above) included drug addicts and lesbians. Monique (left), an inmate befriended by Gabrielle.

room and subjected to the dreaded "sleep treatment", where the patient drifts into a drug-induced coma for days on end. Christian underwent two "cures", each lasting three weeks. He was only wakened for meals, which he ate while half-conscious. Theoretically, the patient emerges from a sleep cure refreshed and relaxed, with all his worries left behind. But more often than not, the result is an acute period of depression, sometimes leading to suicide.

Christian's only "madness" was his love for Gabrielle. Yet he was being treated like the victim of some acute neurosis. After two months at the clinic, he finally broke and agreed not to see Gabrielle again. The promise extracted in the clinic, however, failed to withstand the clearer air of freedom. Once outside, Christian broke his word and ran back to his lover. But things had changed. Christian's further defiance of his parents and the law

meant that Gabrielle was bound to be jailed again. She refused to meet him. "Do what you like," she told him over the telephone, her voice tired and resigned.

Two days later—after she had arranged to have her twin children cared for—Gabrielle was committed to the Les Baumettes jail in Marseilles, cell No. 13. The only concession Gabrielle was allowed to share a cell with two, instead of three, other women. They were both lesbians.

Life at its most raw

Gabrielle, the scholar and academic, was no longer even a human being with a name. Her number was 59264. With her short hair and boyish figure, she was branded as a lesbian by the other women in the prison. The guards shouted obscene remarks after her—most of them to do with her and Christian. From the cultured world of poetry and literature, Gabrielle was plunged into life at its most raw. Tragically, she was not built for it.

Although the press and the intellectual fringe still supported her, grassroots public opinion had finally turned against Gabrielle. She had dared to challenge the most sacred of French ideals—the family unit, and the right of a father to impose obedience and discipline on his children. Hundreds of letters poured into the prison — mostly from parents — demanding that Gabrielle should remain behind bars.

Not that there was any question of releasing her. The authorities were again playing their favourite cat-and-mouse game of dangling Gabrielle's liberty as a bait for Christian. Once again, it worked. Christian gave himself up and Gabrielle was immediately freed. The prison ordeal had shattered her already frail physique and affected her mind. Her ex-husband, Michel Nogues, was shocked when he met her at the prison gates. Her reactions were those of a whipped dog. She trembled uncontrollably and flinched at any loud noise or sudden movement. In the following weeks, neighbours frequently found her cowering in her darkened flat, sobbing and moaning. Once she was discovered huddled behind the refrigerator. She also made her first attempt at suicide, with an overdose of sleeping pills.

On July 10, 1969, three weeks after leaving prison, she stood trial on the original charge of *Détournement de Mineur*. The hearing was held behind locked doors. Right from the start, it was clear that there was going to be no question of leniency. In a merciless legal manoeuvre, the Public Prosecutor asked for a suspended sentence of 13 months. This was to make sure that Gabrielle could not benefit from the general amnesty about to be granted by the authorities to all those awaiting sentences of less than 12 months.

It was not so much the punishment that was harsh. Failure to secure the amnesty would mean that Gabrielle would have an official prison record. And that would be enough for the Ministry of Education to ban her from teaching in any French school for the rest of her life. The authorities were going to be satisfied with nothing less than the complete destruction of her career. But it wasn't so easy.

To the barely concealed disgust of the prosecution, the Presiding Judge gave Gabrielle a 12-month suspended sentence, with a fine of $100. Gabrielle's joy and relief, however, lasted only 30 minutes. Before she had even left the court, the Public Prosecutor entered an appeal against the leniency of the sentence. Only 10 such appeals had been made in the last 40 years of French justice. The authorities were determined not to let Gabrielle off the legal hook.

"She deserved it"

Observers detected the hand of the Ministry of Education in the decision — a view reinforced by the Deputy Prosecutor, who explained later: "An inscription on her police record was needed so as to facilitate disciplinary action and remove her from her post. She deserved it."

But did she? In the welter of public comment, two fairly valid points were made: that Gabrielle had abused her responsibilities as a teacher, and that she had broken the rigidly upright code of

NEIGHBOURS (right) smelled gas but "didn't know what was going on" when Gabrielle died, her spirit broken, in her 11th-floor flat (above). Christian's virile appearance might have swayed the judges, but he was never called.

Both Domenech

behaviour expected from a State employee.

In the circumstances, it was catastrophic that the one person who could have shed a different light on the affair was not called to the witness-stand . . . Christian Rossi. Only he could have convinced the judges that his passion had been as strong as Gabrielle's. That it had not been a teacher-pupil seduction but a genuine love-affair, based as much as anything else upon intellectual and spiritual qualities. If Christian had admitted to having had other love-affairs, it would have lightened the cloud of national disapproval lowering over Gabrielle. Even his un-childlike appearance—tall, burly and bearded—would have helped. But throughout the entire secret hearing Christian never appeared in the courtroom.

In jail, Gabrielle had written, "Everything I love has been spoiled and dirtied" and, "They have made a mountain out of nothing." The shock of the appeal was too much for her. Now it was Gabrielle's turn for the drastic "sleep cure", followed by the seemingly inevitable period of acute depression, in which she again attempted suicide.

For her, there was nothing more to hope for, nothing left to look forward to. Just another trial, and ruin. "I can't go on, Michel . . ." she wrote to her ex-husband from the La Recouvrance rest-home. On the last Saturday of August, 1969, Gabrielle returned to her lonely flat. It was near the end of the summer holidays—when almost the whole of France shuts down and takes its vacation—and Marseilles was a ghost town.

Some time the next day an unknown visitor came and Gabrielle made her guest and herself a cup of coffee. Shortly afterwards, she stuffed all the cracks in the windows and doors with old newspapers and rolled-up clothing, swallowed all her remaining sleeping pills, and turned on the gas. Her body was discovered on Monday.

Absolutely legal

The news of Gabrielle's death sparked off an orgy of self-justification among the authorities. "I as a public minister did nothing more than my job," said the Deputy Prosecutor. "From that point of view, we are all responsible, we are all assassins." An official commented smugly, "Everything we did was absolutely legal and within the law."

Another official even attempted to suggest that it had all been Gabrielle's own fault, because of her superior education. "If she had been a hairdresser, or if she had slept with a young apprentice, it would have been different," he said. Even Gabrielle's severest critics agreed that,

A WELTER of public comment . . . then an orgy of self-justification among the authorities. From jail Gabrielle wrote: "Everything I love has been spoiled and dirtied."

if she had been a man, the charges would never have been brought.

The Ministry of Education's touching little condolence was a bill for two months' salary, to cover the time Gabrielle had been away from work and in prison. With their mother's death, the debt was inherited by Gabrielle's two children, Joel and Valerie.

Like one of the doomed romantic heroines in the classical literature she loved, Gabrielle had paid for her passion with her life. But in the same way that the great lovers of literature are immortal, the uneasy memory of Gabrielle's persecution has not blurred and faded like many another French *cause célèbre*.

The affair of Gabrielle Russier still arouses passionate argument in France. Prophetically, two chalked slogans—scrawled by angry students—stayed on the door of her flat for months after her death. One was "Immortal Gatito". The other was the Greek letter Z, meaning "he lives". And on the street outside, her car still stood unattended, proclaiming to every passer-by "Make Love, Not War".

THE night had been stormy and rain-lashed, with thunder and lightning enveloping the small Suffolk village of Peasenhall. At eight o'clock the following morning—Sunday, June 1, 1902—a local carpenter called William Harsent trudged through the sodden streets to Providence House—the home of Deacon and Mrs. Crisp.

Harsent was bringing some clean linen for his 23-year-old daughter, Rose, who worked there as a maid. She had her own bedroom leading off upstairs from the kitchen, and her father entered the house by the kitchen door, softly calling out her name. He got no reply, moved towards the staircase, and then froze with horror. Lying with her face to the wall, her body supported by the bottom step, was the blood-drenched body of Rose—her nightdress scarlet from her wounds.

Mr. Harsent forced himself to stoop and feel the dead girl's hands. They were quite cold, and turning her head slightly he saw that her throat had been

WILLIAM GARDINER

cut—as a doctor later put it—"from ear to ear".

The alarm was given, the police arrived, and Constable Eli Nunn noted a number of other things about Rose. Her breasts and buttocks had also been slashed, a broken lamp and candlestick lay nearby, the hem of her nightdress was burnt, a copy of the previous day's *East Anglian Daily Times* was underneath her head. Most significant of all, a smashed medicine bottle was near the remains bearing a label saying: "Two teaspoonfuls to be taken every four hours—Mrs. Gardiner's chdn (children)."

Immediately Constable Nunn—and everyone else in Peasenhall who learnt about the bottle—associated it with William Gardiner, a master carpenter and father of six children, who lived with his wife and family in a stone cottage

ROSE HARSENT (above and left) was found brutally murdered at Providence House. Was her chapel-going lover, William Gardiner (below), also her killer?

some 200 yards from Providence House.

For some time he had been suspected of "carrying on" with the dead girl (two local youths had seen him "behaving indecently" with her in a chapel on the outskirts of the village), and letters found in a box beside Rose's bed confirmed their liaison. "Dear R," said one, "I will try to see you tonight at twelve o'clock at your place if you put a light in your window. . . . Do not have a light in your room at twelve, as I will come round to the back."

A second letter stated, "I was very much surprised . . . to hear that there is some scandal going around about you and me going into the . . . chapel." While a third read: "I have broken the news to Mrs. Gardiner . . . and she is awfully upset . . . she knows it is wrong." The letter arranging the rendezvous had been delivered to Rose in a yellow envelope on the afternoon of Saturday, May 31.

But the most sensational revelation was yet to come. Rose Harsent was pregnant and had admitted it to her employer two weeks before. There was only one candidate for the father: William Gardiner.

The police discovered that a light from Rose's bedroom window could be seen

VIRILE, devout — and married — carpenter Gardiner (pictured in front of Ipswich Assize Court after re-trial) made a good impression on judge and jury.

without difficulty at Gardiner's cottage, and a gamekeeper named Morris declared that on the morning of June 1 he had come across some footprints leading from the cottage to the kitchen gate of Providence House. The prints were peculiar in that the india-rubbered soles had horizontal bars across the treads.

It was established that Gardiner possessed such a pair of boots, and a neighbour of his stated that he had seen the carpenter (and his wife) up early that Sunday morning "working in the wash-house". It was assumed that blood was being removed from Gardiner's clothing, he was arrested, and his trial opened at Suffolk Assizes at Ipswich on November 7.

From the start, the carpenter's appearance made a firm impression on the jury. Aged 34, upright, with clear eyes and hair so black that he was said to be of Spanish origin, he looked what he was: a virile married man and a devout chapelgoer.

He showed no signs of distress or panic, not even when Harry Burgess, a

Peasenhall bricklayer, told the court that he had met Gardiner in front of his cottage at about five to ten on the night of May 31. They chatted for a while about local happenings, then Burgess glanced in the direction of Deacon Crisp's house. "From where I stood," he said, "I could see Providence House and noticed a light in the top east window."

None of this shook Gardiner's story — that he had only known Rose slightly through their attendance of the Methodist chapel, that he had not written any letters to her (despite the fact that the yellow envelope was similar to those used by his employer in the village), and that (despite a copy of the paper he took being found beneath the body) he had not visited Providence House on that or any other night. The police had found no blood on his boots, and the only time he had had blood on his knife or his person was after he'd been out "hulking", or disembowelling, rabbits.

His wife confirmed this and, taking her place in the witness-box, declared that her married life was happy, that she had a "good and faithful" husband. She stated that she and Gardiner had gone to bed late on the night in question, after visiting one of their neighbours.

Although her husband had slept soundly, she had not. "More than once" the sound of the storm had awoken her, and she had gone to comfort one of the children who was ill and frightened. The theme of Gardiner the righteous but gravely wronged man was taken up by his lawyer, Mr. Ernest Wild, when he told the jury:

"It did not much matter to him [Gardiner] whether there was another added to the army of martyrs by an unjust condemnation; happen what might, he was a ruined man. He who had held such a proud position in the workshop and in the chapel — who had been in the habit of calling his children to his knee, and teaching them the elements of the Gospel — would never recover from the shadow that had been cast upon his reputation."

When the jurors returned after two hours it was to report that they could not reach a unanimous verdict: 11 of them considered Gardiner guilty, 1 did not. In January 1903, a second trial was held, and once again the jury could not come to a unanimous decision. The evidence against Gardiner was not strong enough; it could have been that Rose had accidentally fallen down the stairs and died that way. A free man again, the carpenter returned to his wife and children, but did not stay long in Peasenhall. He and his family moved to a London suburb, where he opened a shop in his own name. And the Peasenhall mystery — the identity of Rose Harsent's lover and murderer — remained unsolved.

THE SURGEON WHO SEVERED HIS WIFE

Dr. Buck Ruxton was given to violent outbursts of rage directed, invariably, at his wife. Once she left him, but was persuaded to return. Then, in September 1935, she disappeared altogether and was never seen again—at least not in one piece. Her skilful husband's surgery had seen to that . . .

AMONG HIS friends in Edinburgh Captain Buck Hakim cut something of a dash. He was good looking, courteous, and had all the charm of a Parsee of excellent family — in 1927 men of his race were something of a rarity in Edinburgh medical circles.

His name was a deliberate joke on his part. It was intended to hint at glamorous Persian origins, and planned as more acceptable to dour Scotsmen than his rightful name of Bukhtyar Rustomji Ratanji Hakim. In the past this had been reduced to Hakim Hakim — or the Parsee equivalent of Mister Mister.

Buck Hakim was born in Bombay in 1899 of doting and respectable parents. He was well educated and 23 years later duly qualified in Bombay University as a Bachelor of Medicine — and, shortly afterwards, as Bachelor of Surgery. A brilliant career was foreseen for him since he gained first class honours in medicine, midwifery, and gynaecology. He went from university to a Bombay hospital, then became Medical Officer to the Malaria Commission.

He could not settle down, however, and joined the Indian Medical Service — which

sent him to Basra and Baghdad. Later he switched to being a ship's doctor and, with a grant from the Bombay Medical College, then attended courses at London's University College Hospital. He followed this with a brief spell in Paris (a city whose ways and morals were much to his liking) before finally settling in the mecca of medicine, Edinburgh.

He was a born neurotic, an emotional hysteric, capable of waves of wild excitement, jealousy, and violent rages. It was on a high tide of romance that he met a charming and kindly Scotswoman, Isa-

DISMEMBERED . . . Ruxton's wife, Mrs. Isabella Ruxton (far left), and nursemaid Mary Jane Rogerson (left). They flank the other members of the shattered family: their three children. Background picture shows the house where Ruxton lived, worked and carved up his wife.

bella Van Ess. She had been briefly married to, and was divorced from, a Dutchman; it was under her maiden name of Kerr that Hakim knew her when she was a restaurant manageress in Edinburgh. Their courtship was stormy but affectionate, and they decided to live together as man and wife.

The young doctor was full of plans, and decided to change his name by deed poll to Buck Ruxton ("It sounds nice," he wrote to a friend. "It trips off the tongue"). He was admitted by the General Medical Council with the right to practise because of his excellent Bombay degrees – although, in fact, he never gained a British degree.

The Ruxtons' life together was a wild one. They were passionately devoted, but spent much time in venomous quarrels and emotional reunions. Ruxton was to say: "We were the kind of people who could not live with each other and could not live without each other . . ."

Uneven relationship

Somehow their uneven relationship their partings and their comings together again, managed to endure. In 1929 Mrs. Ruxton was expecting a child, and the next year she and Ruxton – and tiny Elizabeth, whom he adored – moved south of the border to the English city of Lancaster. There, in a solid terrace house, 2 Dalton Square, Ruxton put up his plate and took over an existing practice.

At last there appeared to be peace. The Ruxtons employed a cook; became the proud parents of another daughter whom they named Diane; and then a third child came along which was born dead. This so upset Isabella that she tried to kill herself, and Ruxton, never a calm man, gave way to an attack of hysterical violence.

As long as he was working hard, he seemed normal, and readily agreed to employ a nursemaid for the children, Mary Jane Rogerson. Her presence, however, did nothing to soothe his constant outbursts – which became so terrifying that Mrs. Ruxton, although she said her children needed her, fled alone to stay with her sister in November 1934.

However, she was soon brought back by an excited, threatening, and cajoling Buck Ruxton – who alternately swore his love for her and then furiously accused her of having been unfaithful to him. The household was at a constant level of uproar, with hardly a day passing without upsets of one sort or another. This chaos of meetings, separations, love, hatred, and

Mirrorpic

melodramatic threats came to a head in September 1935.

A Miss Susan Johnson was walking peacefully along a road outside Moffat on the main road to Edinburgh, enjoying the fresh autumn air and the quietness of a Sabbath afternoon. She reached a little stone bridge over a stream known as Gardenholme Linn, and bent over to look at the slowly moving water, quiet after the recent storms.

Gruesome jigsaw

Suddenly she tensed at something she saw and hurried back to the hotel where she was staying. There she told her brother what she had seen. Together with a friend, he ran down to the water, and stared in disbelief at a human hand sticking out of paper wrapping. Nearby were bundles of newspaper and sheeting containing what looked like parts of a human body.

The police, too, were staggered at what they found that day (and on days following) – bundles of newspaper, torn bed

linen, a blouse, a pair of child's rompers, bits of straw and cotton-wool, all containing no fewer than 70 portions of human remains, decomposing and maggot infested. Next, a left foot was found by the roadside some miles away and, finally, a right forearm and hand by another road.

When put together, the gruesome jigsaw comprised a body, but with the whole trunk missing; and a second body almost complete except for the right foot. It was a well contrived butchery, expertly designed to make sure that identification was not possible (all the natural protuberances of both heads had been removed, together with skin and many of the teeth).

The wave of shock which hit Britain contained a certain amount of disbelief — people could not accept that such a savage thing had happened, and the newspapers echoed the prevailing incredulity.

Two days later Professor John Glaister (author of the classic *Medical Jurisprudence*) and a small team of doctors set out to crack the apparently unsolvable case. The remains were reassembled into two bodies, both female, and the measurements from certain long bones and other details enabled the heights, weights, ages, and possible appearance of the bodies when living to be charted.

But there the medical men — who had reconstructed *portraits parlé* of two nearly recognizable women from the rotting remains — had to stop. They could offer no clues as to the actual identities of the corpses.

Meanwhile, the police were following up such leads as they had — such as pieces of newspaper, which at first sight seemed useless. There was a segment of a *Daily Herald* for August 6, 1935, stuck to one of the heads; a month later another portion of the same paper was found containing a foot. Parts of a *Sunday Chronicle* had been used as a shroud of sorts, and last and most important of all was a sheet of a *Sunday Graphic* dated September 15, 1935.

It was a slip edition — a special printing containing a local event which the Manchester office had included to boost nearby sales. The slip dealt with a carnival at the Lancashire seaside resort of Morecambe — and had been on sale only there, in the neighbouring countryside, and in Lancaster, some four miles away.

Enquiries showed that no one in or around Morecambe appeared to be missing. It was therefore decided to widen the search and concentrate on people who had been missing since before September 19. Detectives descended upon Lancaster, but were faced with quite a problem. Apart from the 40,000 inhabitants of the town, there were numerous holiday-makers. If nobody was found to be missing, the murder squad would be back to square one.

Then chance stepped into the picture. The Chief Constable of Dumfriesshire, in Scotland, happened to see a local newspaper which mentioned the "disappearance", on October 1, of a young local woman — Mary Jane Rogerson. The missing girl's mother was approached, and the blouse and rompers were shown to her. This paid off. Mrs. Rogerson positively identified the blouse as one she had made for her daughter. More than that, she mentioned a lady who had given a pair of child's rompers to Mary Rogerson. The rompers, too, were positively identified — by means of a peculiar knot in the supporting elastic.

Insanely jealous

The net now began to close, and it seemed as if Ruxton was trying to draw it around himself. On October 10 he went to the Lancaster police asking if "discreet enquiries could be made with a view to finding my wife". Detectives then investigated the doctor's background, and some very curious facts were revealed.

Ruxton had given out that his wife and the nursemaid were away (a story that varied with different people). On the day they had supposedly gone on their journey he asked a neighbour to look after the children as, he claimed, he had badly cut his hand. Displaying a large bandage, he then employed two women to come and scrub down the bath and staircase and clean some rolled-up carpets in his house.

After throwing buckets of water on the carpets, the women noticed that "the colour of the water that came off was like blood". What had obviously happened was that Ruxton, in one of his insanely jealous rages, had killed his wife — and then butchered Mary Rogerson so that she could not inform on him. It is clear that Mrs. Ruxton had received violent blows on the face and was strangled — while Mary Rogerson's skull was frac-

DROPPED over the ravine (left), the bodies came to rest beneath the bridge at the spot marked X (above left). The doctor's disposal methods appear to have lacked the sophistication of his surgery!

AP, Mirrorpic

tured and she had probably been killed with a knife.

On the week-end of the murders the cook had been given time off, and Ruxton had set about destroying—or at least dissecting—the bodies. It was a major task, and he approached it with all his skill and experience as a surgeon. He had carefully removed his dead wife's fingerprints, but with typical lack of logic had failed to obliterate those of Miss Rogerson—which were later found to match those of body No. 1.

Then—after Professor Glaister had shown that plaster casts made of the feet of the two partly reconstructed bodies filled the shoes worn by the two "missing" women—he produced his masterstroke and proved the identity of one of the corpses beyond any doubt.

Taking an already existing photograph of Mrs. Ruxton's head—and enlarging it to life size—he placed over it a negative of the skull of the older body. Even to laymen it could be seen that the two matched—the contours were exact, the orifices of mouth and eyes could not be faulted. A number of tiny parallels and measurements fully satisfied him that the second body was that of Mrs. Isabella Ruxton.

However, it was not necessarily *legal* proof of identity. At most it was strong supporting evidence, but the law requires facts that cannot be disputed by a clever defence counsel. Fortunately for the police and prosecution there was more: vaccination marks, a bunion, and other small physical factors which spelled the gallows for the murderous Parsee.

From the blood in Ruxton's house, from witnesses, and from the endlessly probing police enquiries the damning facts were built up. The doctor appeared at Manchester Assizes in the spring of 1936, when the only witness called for the defence was the accused himself. He wept and made hysterical outbursts. He swore to his innocence, shouting that all he knew was that his wife and Mary Rogerson had left the house together, and he had not seen them again alive or dead.

"That is absolute bunkum, with a capital B!" he cried to the prosecution's assertion that he had dismembered his two victims in the privacy of his house. But the judge, in his summing-up, concluded: "Could anything be clearer?"

The jury took an hour to bring in a verdict of guilty. After his appeal was dismissed, Dr. Buck Ruxton was hanged at Strangeways Jail, Manchester, on May 12, 1936. He left a sealed letter confessing to both murders with a journalist, to be opened in the event of his death.

TASK COMPLETED! Prosecuting counsel Maxwell Fyfe, with briefcase and furled umbrella, and jurymen (top), return home after the verdict of guilty.

LUCKY LUCIANO

The Mafia existed in New York for many years before the police recognized its existence. The law knew there were gangs but were unaware how well they were organized. Lucky Luciano knew the real power of the Mafia – he joined the Mob in 1919 and by the 1930s was ready to take it into a new dimension, always one step ahead of the law.

Young Blood

The Nuovo Villa Tammaro Restaurant (above), where Joe Masseria ate his last meal. Its owner, Gerardo Scarpato, was well known for his fine cuisine.

Gangland killings were nothing new in New York between the wars, but 1931 saw two major assassinations that were to change the face of the Mafia. The man behind them had big ambitions.

Joe 'the Boss' Masseria was a short, but powerfully-built, middle-aged man who, by 1931, had been the most powerful gangster in New York for a decade. On 15 April 1931, he drove his steel-armoured sedan, which had plate-glass an inch thick in all its windows, to Coney Island, the seaside resort in New York's Brooklyn borough.

Unusually for him, the boss was alone. He was not expecting danger, for he was to eat at a favourite Italian restaurant with two of his most trusted younger lieutenants. His lunch companions were the brutal Vito Genovese and a dark young gangster with a drooping right eyelid, who was known as 'Lucky' Luciano. These men had recently outlined plans to Masseria for eliminating a score of mobsters who worked for an up-and-coming rival gang led by Salvatore Maranzano.

The meal was as good as Masseria had hoped. He ate his way through hot and cold antipasti, minestrone soup, a seafood salad, Lobster Fra Diavolo, Spaghetti alla Milanese and a mouthwatering selection of pastries. Luciano, for his part, ate more sparingly, and only sipped at the many imported Italian wines on offer. When they eventually ordered coffees, the meal had already lasted for three hours.

The restaurant had been crowded when the gangsters began eating, but by 3.00 p.m. all the other customers had left. Genovese pleaded urgent business back in central New York and departed. Restaurant owner Gerardo Scarpato decided that he felt like a walk along the beach. Luciano, alone with Masseria now, suggested that the boss might like a game of cards. Masseria agreed to a hand. It was almost 3.30 p.m.

Luciano excused himself to go to the men's room. At almost exactly the same moment, a black limousine, driven by veteran gangster Ciro Terranova, drew up in front of the restaurant. Terranova remained at the wheel as four men jumped out. Vito Genovese had returned, with Joe Adonis, Albert Anastasia and Benny 'Bugsy' Siegel. All were friends of Luciano and, like him, were young, ruthless men. Men who thought that the old guard had had their day.

Masseria hardly had time to react. The four gangsters unleashed a fusillade of more than 20 bullets into his back. Masseria slumped over the table, a river of his blood mingling with the remains of his last meal.

After completing their work, which took less than a minute, the four rushed out of the restaurant to the waiting car. But Ciro Terranova, who had gone in awe of Joe the Boss, was too nervous to put the car into gear. Contemptuously, 'Bugsy' Siegel, the handsome young Jewish mobster and noted killer, shoved Terranova out of the way and drove the car away at top speed.

When the killers had gone, Lucky Luciano stepped back into the restuarant to survey what was really his own handiwork. He had passed the stage when he would himself pull the

> ## Oh, of course, my good friend, Lucky. I will be right here when you return . . . and perhaps I give you another chance to beat me at cards
>
> JOE MASSERIA, just before his death

trigger on his victims, as he had done in his younger days. Now he waited quietly beside the corpse until the police arrived. It was a clear demonstration to the underworld that Luciano had taken another step on his road to kingship of New York crime.

When the police arrived, Luciano affected total ignorance of what had

Joe Adonis (left) was one of the team of Mafia hitmen who shot Joe 'the Boss' Masseria. Adonis had known Luciano in their early days on the Lower East Side. He became one of Luciano's trusted sidekicks, running gambling clubs in New York and bookmaking at the racetracks. His real surname was Doto, but he was always known as Adonis, on account of his good looks.

VITO GENOVESE

IN CONTEXT

Vito Genovese, at first an ally and later a bitter enemy of Lucky Luciano, was born three days before him in Naples in 1897. When the two men first discovered this, they were delighted, and for many years held a joint birthday party.

Vito Genovese was a particularly brutal hitman whose killings were not confined to gangsters. When Genovese fell in love with the beautiful Anna Vernotico in 1932, he killed her husband Gerard to marry her. Later Anna sued for an expensive divorce and informed on the Mafia, but 'Don Vitone' loved her too much to have her eliminated. Instead, he killed Steve Franse, the man who had become her lover.

*The view from
40th Street,
looking up Park
Avenue (left). The
building in the
middle of the
picture, with
statues and a
clock, is Grand
Central Station.
Salvatore
Maranzano, who
became head of
the Mafia upon
Masseria's death,
had his office in
Park Avenue near
the station. It was
here that he was
killed. His killers
escaped through
the station.*

Popperfoto

MAFIA WARS

BACKGROUND

The Castellammarese Wars were between the rival Mafia mobs led by Joe Masseria and Salvatore Maranzano. Maranzano and many of his mob came from Castellammare del Golfo in Sicily. Masseria, however, was from Naples and his gang also included mainland Italians.

Younger gangsters, such as Luciano, saw the wars as a process by which Masseria and Maranzano would eliminate each other, after which Italian and Jewish mobsters (who were excluded from the Mafia) would cooperate to build a modern Mafia.

The wars were sparked off, late in 1929, by the defection of Tom Reina from Masseria to Maranzano. Reina was an important gang leader in the Bronx. On 26 February 1930, Luciano, Masseria's lieutenant, sent Vito Genovese to kill Reina, in order to strengthen the Masseria organization. Luciano's motive for tipping the balance of power in favour of Joe Masseria was to strengthen his own hand. He reasoned that, at a later date, he could offer Masseria's head to Salvatore Maranzano. His price for betraying his master would be his appointment as number two in Maranzano's undisputed gangster empire.

happened. He was reported to have said, 'As soon as I had finished drying my hands, I walked out to see what it was all about.' This was a rather polished version of the mobster's usual style of speech. What he actually said, in the rasping accent of the Lower East Side, was, 'I was in the can taking a leak. I always take a long leak.'

> " **I never really liked him, but he did have moxie. He could fight like a son of a bitch. I didn't have to love him to use him**
>
> LUCKY LUCIANO on Vito Genovese
> "

That was not the only re-arrangement of the facts that went on after the Masseria assassination. A famous press photo showed the dead Masseria still holding the Ace of Diamonds in his right hand. Legend has it that Masseria had been about to beat Luciano in the game they were playing. In reality, the photographer placed the card in Masseria's hand to get a dramatic picture.

Masseria was given a send-off that befitted his status. His body lay in state for several days and was eventually taken to the cemetery accompanied by many lavish floral tributes and a huge convoy of mourners in their limousines. Among them was the

sober-suited Luciano.

But Luciano was not yet the Boss of all Bosses, the *capo di tutti capi*. This honour now belonged to Salvatore Maranzano, a man older than Masseria. Maranzano had been born in 1868 and had only come to the USA in the 1920s, after a long career in the Mafia of Sicily. He was a differ-

ent type of man from the crude, foul-mouthed, powerfully-built Masseria. Maranzano had trained for the priesthood and was fond of making quotations in Latin. He fancied himself as an expert on Julius Caesar, and, like Caesar, he was determined to be number one.

Maranzano lost no time in calling a massive banquet and conference at which his position as *capo di tutti capi*, at least in New York, could be officially ratified. Every mafioso had to pay six dollars to attend. Luciano, the crown prince, sat at Maranzano's right hand. Raising a clenched fist, Maranzano proclaimed himself supreme ruler. From now on, he said, crime in New York would be run by five 'families', one of which Luciano was to lead. Each family would have a boss, an underboss, a group of *caporegime* (district leaders) and soldiers under them in groups of ten.

Maranzano's division of the mobsters into something like Julius Caesar's legions was one of his more creative strokes. His organizational structure was to long outlive his own four-month reign as *capo*, and it was soon extended to the rest of the USA.

Maranzano was, at base, a bloodthirsty and hidebound old Sicilian. Very soon, sensing dissension in the ranks, he was planning a wholesale massacre of the men he had just confirmed as leaders of the families. In New York, Luciano and Genovese were prime targets, while in Chicago, he planned to dispose of Al Capone. Maranzano hired a non-Italian killer, Vincent 'Mad Dog' Coll, for the contract on Luciano and Genovese.

Luciano and Genovese were soon tipped off about the old Don's intentions. They decided to knock off Maranzano at exactly the moment he

> ## "
> ## The way they talk about my lieutenants, I got more than the army
> LUCKY LUCIANO
> "

planned to eliminate them. They commissioned Meyer Lansky to hire a team of four Jewish killers, headed by 'Red' Levine, a strict Jew who always wore a yarmulke under his hat when he went out on a job on the Sabbath. These men were instructed to pose as federal tax agents in order to gain access to Maranzano's heavily guarded office on Park Avenue, behind Grand Central Station. Maranzano was proud of paying his taxes.

It was the afternoon of 10 September 1931. Maranzano had summoned Luciano and Genovese to his office. He was a little disconcerted when, shortly before they and 'Mad Dog' Coll were due to arrive, a visit was announced from tax inspectors. Only when the four-man team lined up Maranzano's secretary and five-strong bodyguard against the wall in the outer office did it become evident this was no tax query. Peering out from his office, Maranzano rushed for the gun in his drawer. But it was too late. The hitmen stabbed him six times, shot him four times and cut his throat.

The killers raced out of the build-

ing, but got separated. 'Bo' Weinberg lost his way on a stairwell, hid in a ladies' toilet and finally emerged on to the concourse at Grand Central Station, where he dropped his gun into the pocket of a commuter going home. 'Red' Levine used the main exit and almost collided with 'Mad Dog' Coll, who was on his way in for the Luciano killing. 'Beat it, Vince, the cops are coming,' Levine warned.

And now the Luciano years were beginning, a period of five years when he was the undisputed king of New York crime. He kept the Maranzano structure, adding new rules of his own, and helped found the National Crime Commission.

THE SICILIAN VESPERS
IN CONTEXT

For many years it was believed that the afternoon of Maranzano's death was followed by a nationwide 'Night of the Sicilian Vespers', in which up to 50 old guard Mafia men were eliminated on Luciano's orders.

It now seems that this is an almost total myth. The only murder that can be verified that night was that of Gerardo Scarpato (funeral shown below), the restaurant owner who had provided Joe Masseria's last meal. Luciano probably felt more comfortable without a non-gangster witness to that incident.

UPI/Bettmann Newsphotos

THE HUSTLER

UPI/Bettmann Newsphotos

Young Lucky arrived in New York from Sicily at the age of nine. He was one of many who made their way to the slums of the Lower East Side. He soon decided that crime was the best way out.

At the turn of the century, immigrants from all parts of Europe were landed at Ellis Island (left), in Upper New York Bay. From there many went to join friends or family in the Lower East Side (above).

Lucky Luciano's real name was Salvatore Lucania. He was born on 24 November 1897, in the village of Lercara Friddi in the hills near Palermo. It was a poor place, where the children played in unpaved streets amid the grey dust and smell of the nearby sulphur mines. Salvatore's father, Antonio Lucania, worked in these mines.

At this time, around the turn of the century, many poor Italians, as well as Jews

from Eastern Europe, were leaving for a better life in the USA. Antonio and Rosalie Lucania had five children, three boys and two girls. The young Salvatore was their middle child.

The family took the steamship from Palermo to New York in 1906. They moved into a crumbling tenement on the Lower East Side, a district jam-packed with Italians, Irish and Jews. Antonio's wages as a day-labourer left him not much better off than he had been

in Sicily. Life was tough and was dominated by street gangs.

From the start, Salvatore hated school and the 'old broads' (he never learnt their names) who taught him in a language he could hardly understand. Aged 12, he was already hustling on the streets and running errands for older criminals. A four-month spell locked up in truant school did nothing to improve him.

At the age of 14, Salvatore was showing a

friend the new gun he had recently acquired. It accidentally went off and Salvatore was hit – the only gunshot wound he ever received. At that age, too, he first took opium, supplied to him by a crooked dentist known as Doc, who was shortly afterwards killed by an addict he had cheated.

Antonio Lucania soon realized that his son was hanging around with 'no-goods', and he frequently beat him. After a particularly severe beating, Salvatore stopped coming home and took to sleeping in empty apartments and pool halls. Around 1913, when he was 16, he began frequenting Martinghetti's Pool Hall in the Lower East Side's notorious Mulberry Bend.

Gang fights

He was a darkly handsome young man, bursting with violence, and he soon came to the notice of the gangsters who controlled Little Italy. Crime was small-time stuff in those days, the Italian Five Points Gang fighting it out block by block with the Jewish gang of Monk Eastman. Joe Masseria, who had just taken over as boss of Little Italy, may have been the one first to notice Lucania.

In those early days, Lucania was used as a gun-

In the New York of 1919 a well-to-do could look forward to a career in business. Many others were not so lucky.

man. He probably carried out more than 20 killings, before rising to a position where he could commission others to kill. His fellow mobster Frank Costello remembers how violent he was and how he himself was once nearly knifed by Lucania.

The young Lucania built up friendships and alliances with the men who would later be his fellow leaders in Crime Incorporated. Many of them came from the Lower East Side.

While still at school, Lucania ran an extortion racket against Jewish children, and the story goes that one boy who refused to be intimidated was the small but very tough Meyer Lansky.

Trusted allies

Lucania was later to choose Lansky as a trusted lieutenant, and what seems to have been a genuinely close friendship between the two men lasted until Lucania's

THE EARLY NY MAFIA

The Mafia began in New York in a small way in the 1880s. Many of its members operated an extortion racket called the Black Hand. The earliest Mafia 'family' were the Morellos, who really were relations. Peter 'the Clutching Hand' Morello, the last important member of this family, was eliminated during the

Castellammarese Wars in the late 1920s.

Ignazio 'the Wolf' Saietta, who was related by marriage to the Morellos, was one of the most feared men in the early days. Under the protection of Paul Kelly's Five Points Gang, 'the Wolf' ran the notorious 'Murder Stable', where he systematically tortured and murdered his victims. He later retired from the Mafia, went into small-time business, and died a natural death in 1944.

Johnny Torrio, who was known as the statesman of the Mafia, was one of the most important men in the early New York Mafia. He understood that violence should only be used when appropriate. Torrio was responsible for the training of a generation of mobsters, including Lucky Luciano, Vito Genovese and Al Capone.

death. Benny 'Bugsy' Siegel, Meyer's tall and handsome partner, was another ally. A little later, Lucania became associated with several other men who would be important in his story: Frank Costello, Joe Adonis and Vito Genovese.

In June 1916, Lucania tried to sell a half-dram of heroin for older gangsters and was arrested outside a pool hall. He said nothing, and was sentenced to a year in Hampton Farms Penitentiary. The regime there was typical of the harshness of United States prisons at that time: he spent hours cleaning toilets, while guards periodically hit him with rubber hoses.

Before going to Hampton Farms, Lucania had taken a job for a few months as a messenger boy for the Goodman Hat Company on West 24th Street. It was the only honest work he ever did. His Jewish employer, Max Goodman, took to the

young Salvatore, falling for his undoubted charm.

Goodman mounted a campaign for Lucania's early release from prison but he did not intend to change his ways. Goodman repeatedly offered him a job but Lucania had decided on a life of crime.

War shy

In 1917, America joined World War I. Although Lucania enjoyed shooting people he was not going to place himself in the line of fire. He deliberately got a dose of syphilis from a prostitute rather than join up. The years of Prohibition were around the corner, years when Lucania's 'career' would really take off.

Although he was frequently quoted as saying, 'I'd die rather than be a crumb,' it would be truer to say Lucania was already a mouldy crumb who would get a lot rottener killing those who stood in his way.

Lucky Days

Popperfoto

Luciano signed up with the US Mafia on the eve of its golden age. Prohibition heralded the start of this era, providing the Mob with a ready-made, illicit but lucrative business throughout the 1920s.

In the summer of 1919, a large number of young Italian-American gangsters joined the Mafia. Among them were Charles Lucania (Lucky Luciano), Vito Genovese and Al Capone, who was shortly to leave New York for Chicago.

No records exist of the ceremony by which Charles Lucania was sworn in, but it was probably similar to the one which former hitman Joe Valachi described when he turned informer in 1963. No doubt Lucania stood amid a circle of older gangsters with a piece of burning paper cupped in his hand and swore to burn like that paper if he ever revealed the secrets of *La Cosa Nostra*, 'this thing of ours'. No doubt he swore also to live and die by the gun and the knife.

On 16 January 1919, Prohibition was ratified and became law a year later. The new law banned the manufacture, sale and transportation of liquor. The moral campaigners of the Women's Christian Temperance Union rejoiced, and so did the gangsters. For ordinary Americans had no intention of becoming teetotal, and they were prepared to award riches, fame and even social acceptance to those who supplied their drinks.

Throughout his career, Lucky Luciano was noted for his ability to co-operate with and learn from Jewish

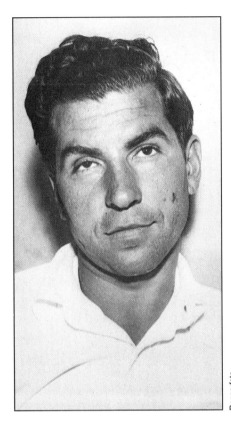

*Lucky Luciano (above) started out
as a small-timer but had become
a top bootlegger by the time
Prohibition ended in 1933. The
fight against bootlegging by city
police, state troopers (left) and
federal agents was at best
half-hearted, because Prohibition
was so unpopular.*

Popperfoto

criminals, and his rise to power took
place because he became the linkman
between top Italian and top Jewish
criminals. In the 1920s, the most notable Jewish mobster was the brilliant
Arnold Rothstein, who was known as
'Mr Fix-it' or 'The Brain'. He was alleged to have fixed the 1919 baseball
World Series. Rothstein, however, had
not immediately seen the opportuni-
ties Prohibition offered. It was Charlie
Lucania who suggested he went into
the imported whisky shipping business. Rothstein also imported narcotics and, by 1921, Lucania had become one of the largest wholesalers in
New York of both commodities.

Hitman

But there was also plenty of business
for Lucania with the Mafia itself. In
the early 1920s, the illegal liquor
market in New York was centred on
the intersection of Mulberry and
Grand Streets, in an area jokingly
called the Curb Exchange (from the
name given to Wall Street stocks not
listed on the Big Board). Joe 'the Boss'
Masseria had his office in a 'social
club' there. Just across the street,
Lucania, who was now known as
Charlie Lucky or Lucky Luciano, set
up his headquarters. Luciano was
Masseria's bodyguard and hitman.
This was the last time in his life when
he was to carry out his own murders.

In the early 1920s, a gang of rival

mobsters, led by Umberto Valenti,
were gunning for Masseria's life. In
August 1922, Masseria gained a reputation in the underworld as someone
who could quite literally dodge bullets
and live. He escaped an ambush, only
to find himself once again caught in
.48-calibre crossfire. He dived into
what he believed was the safety of a
men's hat shop on Second Avenue.
But one of Valenti's men pursued him
to the back of the shop and fired four
shots as Masseria cowered on the
floor. The gunman took two more
shots, and once again missed, before
fleeing.

Short-lived peace

After that, Joe Masseria's reputation
was semi-mythical, but he knew he
had to get Valenti quickly if he
wanted to live much longer. He and
two henchmen, including Luciano,
waited in a doorway at 194 Grand
Street for Valenti and his bodyguard
to appear. Valenti ran off unharmed,
but the bodyguard was hit – he took
two months to die.

Eventually, Masseria summoned
Valenti to a meeting to discuss peace
at a spaghetti house on East 12th

MONEY LENDER

UPI Bettmann Newsphotos

ARNOLD ROTHSTEIN
He lent money to criminal enterprises in return for a share of the profits and a mortgage on the criminal's property. He owned a vast amount of property and was an expert at turning criminal earnings into legitimate fortunes.

Street. With what seems considerable foolhardiness, Valenti agreed to attend. The young Lucky Luciano was Masseria's fellow diner, Valenti was alone. The men enjoyed their meal and seemed to have come to terms. They came out of the restaurant and

Luciano was becoming a power in the New York rackets. However, on 2 June that year, he sold two ounces of morphine to a pusher called John Lyons. What Luciano did not know was that Lyons was a federal informer. Three days later he tried to

> ## "That's where I made my money; I made it in bootlegging and gambling. But dope? I never touched no dope
> LUCKY LUCIANO

walked to a corner. There, two other Masseria men came up and they, together with Luciano, opened fire on Valenti. He was killed trying to get into a taxi.

By early 1923, both as right-hand man to Masseria and as the link with Rothstein and other Jewish gangsters,

sell more morphine to Lyons and was arrested by federal narcotics agents. Luciano seemed certain to be successfully prosecuted, but he struck a bargain to gain his freedom by telling agents where to find a large cache of narcotics belonging to non-Mafia gangsters. There were persistent rumours that he had also turned informer, but this cannot be proved.

Luciano was not yet the powerful, seemingly invulnerable gangster he was to become later. He was still a violent young peasant, someone who had himself tattooed with the name Lucky, who boasted about his fabulous luck and who liked to escort chorus girls to the flashest joints.

Touch of class

Luciano himself gave much of the credit to Rothstein — 'the best etiquette teacher a guy could ever have' — for giving him class and persuading him that a modern, successful gangster is nothing if not discreet. He moved into a large apartment, tastefully furnished, on the Upper East Side, where he would not allow women to stay for more than a single night. Later, about 1927, he moved into a suite at the elegant Barbizon Plaza Hotel, where he was known as Mr Charles Lane, a businessman.

During the mid-1920s, under the stimulus of the enormous business generated by Prohibition, all the underworld rackets were highly profit-

Hulton-Deutsch Collection

Jack 'Legs' Diamond (left centre) was a leading New York bootlegger. He was convicted for having an unlicensed still (opposite page) in New York.

Topham

able. Some of the most lucrative were loansharking, narcotics, the Policy or Numbers gambling game, to which Lansky added some ingenious refinements, and extortion money from the unions, particularly in New York's Garment Center, where the Jewish gangster, Louis 'Lepke' Buchalter, had a hold. In Chicago, it was an era of incredible violence and mayhem, which will be forever associated with the name Al Capone.

Order had to come to crime, and Lucky Luciano was to rise by supplying it. As chief executive of the Masseria empire, he became a leading light in the 'Seven Group', a cartel that controlled bootlegging. Other members included Joe Adonis, who operated in Brooklyn, Lansky and Siegel in New York and King Solomon, who ruled Boston. The group was a forerunner of the sort of unity which would emerge at the Atlantic City Conference of May 1929, the underworld's first great general congress.

Narcotics empire

Violence remained the hallmark of the underworld. On 4 November 1928 came the death of Arnold Rothstein, who was shot in his New York hotel apartment and died later in hospital of his wounds. Rumour had it that he had been killed because he welshed on a gambling debt. Just 30 minutes after

BOOTLEGGING

Arnold Rothstein, the Jewish mobster, was the man who financed many of the leading bootleggers. He put up $175,000 for Waxey Gordon to smuggle boatloads of real Scotch whisky into New York from Canada. The money paid for the whisky, transport and all necessary bribes. Lucky Luciano, 'Legs' Diamond and Dutch Schultz also became major rumrunners, funded by Rothstein's money.

Much of the spirits and beer sold in speakeasies – New York had 30,000 of these bars – was home-made. Moonshiners set up spirit stills and beer vats in old barns and even in city warehouses. They paid for police 'protection' but had to suffer occasional raids for the sake of appearances.

Gangsters ran the speakeasies, bankrolled small producers and made the largest profits.

his death three men were apprehended going through the files in his private office, but they were released. One of them was Charles Lucania, who was described simply as 'a waiter'. Whatever the reason for Rothstein's death, the information Luciano and his colleagues gathered in those vital few minutes enabled him to succeed to Rothstein's narcotics empire.

In October 1929, Luciano escaped with his life in mysterious circumstances. He was 'taken for a ride', a trip that only the rarest gangster survived. Kidnapped at an unknown place, he was severely beaten up, and was eventually found by patrolling policemen as he wandered around dazed in a wooded section of Staten Island, having been dumped on a nearby beach. 'Christ, I thought I was in New Jersey,' he said when they told him where he was.

He claimed not to know who had

beaten him up, and during the rest of his life he told many conflicting versions. We are never likely to know who was responsible. The Castellammarese Wars were just beginning, and one possibility is that rival gangsters carried out the beating. Equally plausible is the theory that detectives took Luciano in and beat him up to make him talk.

'Lucky' legends

The fact that Luciano had survived such a 'ride' did much to bolster his fast-growing reputation. Various legends grew up around the incident. One maintained that he gained the name 'Lucky' Luciano because of this, but the truth is that he had already begun to encourage use of this moniker in the early 1920s.

The days of Luciano's greatest power were just ahead, but he had survived the greatest danger on the threshold of becoming king.

POWER AND CORRUPTION

Through threats and bribery, organized crime corrupts the very people who should be stamping it out. The Mob buys or terrifies those in authority because, once corrupted, they are powerless to act against it.

T he fact that organized crime has become America's largest industry is not solely due to the criminals. Corruption in public office has long been a fact of life in America and still persists, despite many moral crusades to beat crime.

The links between criminals and officially legitimate citizens go back almost to the beginning of American history. In the frontier days of the 19th century, politicians and hoodlums were often virtually indistinguishable: both ruled from the local saloon. Later, in the world of big cities and millions of immigrants, the rich and powerful on both sides of the law conspired to protect each other.

Mob power

The heyday of corruption in New York, when virtually all arms of public service were in the pay of the Mafia, was in the early 1930s, the period when Lucky Luciano held power. The Mayor of New York at this time was Jimmy Walker, a former writer of popular songs. He was firmly in the control of Tammany Hall, the corrupt Democratic political club which had long controlled City Hall. To show what he thought of Prohibition, he held beer parades along Broadway.

His police commissioner,

The end of Prohibition, on 7 April 1933, brought crowds on to the streets to celebrate the return of legitimate 'booze'.

Tammany Hall (above), the Democratic club, became a byword for corruption. Those who ran it were in the pay of the Mob, and their candidates were Mafia puppets.

whom he appointed in 1928, was Grover A. Whalen, the former manager of a department store. He took bribes from gangster Frank Costello to allow Costello to set up illegal slot machines all over the city.

In Mafia pay

The gangsters had another good friend in Tammany Hall boss Jimmy Hines, who was a salaried member of Dutch Schultz's gang and eventually went to prison. Hines called William C. Dodge, the Manhattan district attorney, 'stupid, respectable and my man.'

Martin T. Manton, a senior judge of the US Circuit Court of Appeals, was finally convicted in 1939 of taking bribes from the Mafia. He had reversed a conviction of Louis 'Lepke' Buchalter, which had enabled Buchalter to escape justice for a time.

Corruption became so widespread that there was a reaction against it. In 1933, Fiorello LaGuardia was elected Mayor of New York and he appointed Thomas E. Dewey as special prosecutor against organized crime. City government became honest, several spectacular prosecutions were held, and big claims were made that crime had been beaten. But LaGuardia was followed by Bill O'Dwyer, another mayor in Mafia pay.

In recent decades corruption has continued. The Teamsters, the huge transportation union, became notorious from the late 1950s for their Mafia connections under boss Jimmy Hoffa. Gangster Tony Scotto raised $1 million for New York Governor Carey's 1974 election campaign and later called him as a character witness at his trial.

Large sums of money (inset), that could only have been bribes, passed through Federal Judge Martin T. Manton (above).

Robert Kennedy proved himself a dedicated enemy of the Mafia during his spell as attorney-general in the early 1960s. In the late 1980s, another major campaign against the Mafia led to the jailing of hundreds of mobsters, including many family bosses. In the early 1990s it seems that only the New York Gambinos family is still fully operational.

It would, however, be rash to claim that the Mafia is on the way out. In America, where attitudes to crime and criminals are complex and ambiguous, the death of organized crime cannot be predicted with certainty.

Jimmy Hoffa (left) used Mob heavies and let the Mafia control Union funds. Jailed in 1967, he 'disappeared' in 1975.

Both UPI/Bettmann Newsphotos

Popperfoto

CHOOSING OFFICIALS

In the USA, the method of choosing public officials, especially those concerned with law enforcement, can lend itself to corruption. Police chiefs are generally appointed by mayors, while district attorneys and sheriffs are almost always elected. Even judges are sometimes elected.

This method of selection means that top law enforcement officers have to be politicians firstly, rather than independent, impartial professionals. If they want to retain their job they must either keep powerful sections of the electorate happy or avoid upsetting the political party that has put them in power. Law enforcement officers can therefore have a vested interest in persecuting the weak and not upsetting the 'fat cats' who have the power to put them out of a job.

'Murder Inc'

In the early 1930s, the American underworld, led by
Luciano, became truly organized. Known as Crime Inc,
it had an effective elimination arm called Murder Inc,
but a new prosecutor was out to smash the rackets.

Once Maranzano, the last of the 'old Dons', had been eliminated in September 1931, Luciano was the undisputed ruler of the New York underworld. Determined not to be an autocratic ruler, he realized co-operation was important. He therefore promptly summoned a meeting of the whole American underworld in Chicago, with Al Capone as host.

Then, in the spring of 1933, supported by Johnny Torrio, the elder statesman of Italian-American crime, Luciano called an even more momentous meeting at a Park Avenue hotel in New York. Here he outlined his plans for a nationwide crime syndicate or National Crime Commission. Crime was to have the structure that every huge American business had.

Businesslike

Luciano kept the structure of crime families and extended it nationwide. Each family would be supreme in its own city or area and all would co-operate. A national syndicate council, in which every family had one vote, would sort out any disputes. Some cities were dominated by Jewish criminals – Cleveland had Moe Dalitz's syndicate, for instance – and these were to be recognized on an equal basis. American organized crime from the

Lucky Luciano (far left) had been living in the Barbizon Plaza Hotel since 1927, under the name Charles Lane. The Waldorf-Astoria Towers hotel (right) opened on 1 October 1931, and Luciano moved into one of the new towers, using the name Charles Ross. He took a fully furnished apartment decorated by a top designer. Situated in Manhattan, between Park Avenue and Lexington Avenue, the hotel provided a discreet centre of operations.

AP/Wide World

1930s onwards was effectively an Italian-Jewish combine.

Luciano made other new rules too. A killing of a major figure could only be authorized by a vote of the national syndicate council and, within each family, a proper hearing was required before any ordinary soldier could be eliminated. It did not always work that way, but the structure and rules Luciano established brought a measure of peace to the underworld.

Luciano was the effective head of the underworld, not only in New York but in America as a whole. He lived like a king, moving into suite 39C of the exclusive Waldorf-Astoria Towers hotel, under the name of Charles Ross. He regularly sampled the girls of New York's most celebrated madam, Polly Adler, while keeping as his chief mistress the beautiful showgirl of Russian origin, Gay Orlova. At the height of his power his annual income may have been as much as $800,000 a year.

Contract killers

The National Crime Commission, or Crime Inc, as it was sometimes called, had its fearsome enforcement arm, Murder Inc. About half the killers in Murder Inc were Italians and the other half were Jews. The two 'lord high executioners' were Albert Anastasia, a

particularly bloodthirsty Italian, and Louis 'Lepke' Buchalter, a Jew.

Up to 1940, when the activities of Murder Inc were revealed by an informer, it may have been responsible for the contract killings of 1,000 people, mostly criminals within the underworld. It is not possible to link Luciano directly with most of these killings, and yet many must have been carried out on his orders.

Among the underworld killings that can be attributed to Luciano is that of Dutch Schultz, an overlord of the Numbers racket in the Bronx. 'The Dutchman' was in fact of German Jewish origin. He was a latecomer to the rackets, being just a small-time thug and bar-keeper until 1928. Then, with particular ruthlessness, he progressed fast, and in the early 1930s was the major criminal in New

Popperfoto

IN CONTEXT

UPI/Bettmann Newsphotos

ST VALENTINE'S DAY MASSACRE

Al Capone, a brutally raw man in his twenties, became crime overlord of Chicago during the 1920s. His power was disputed by the Irish gangs of Chicago's North side. Their leader, Dion O'Banion, a florist, had been shot on Capone's orders in his shop in 1924. What remained of his gang had passed under the control, in 1929, of George 'Bugs' Moran.

On 14 February 1929, a snowy St Valentine's Day, six of Moran's men were in the garage of the SMC Cartage Company at 2122 North Clark Street awaiting what they thought was a consignment of hijacked Canadian whisky. Also present was Dr Reinhardt Schwimmer, an optometrist, who appears to have been a 'groupie' of the gangsters. Moran was expected, but he had overslept and was late.

When men dressed as policemen entered, the Moran men thought it

was a police raid and allowed themselves to be lined up with their faces to the wall. More men, carrying machine guns, then entered and mowed them down. The killers left with the suspects they had arrested still believing their captors to be policemen.

One of the Moran men, Frank Gusenberg, was alive when found by real policemen, but died later in hospital. In traditional gangland style he refused to name his killers. They were never identified, but there is no doubt they were henchmen of Capone. He himself was in Miami, ostentatiously keeping an appointment with an official, when the massacre happened. However, as Moran said, 'Only Capone kills like that.' Moran had arrived at the garage, seen the murderers' car outside the garage, and promptly departed. He died in prison in 1957.

York who was independent of the syndicate, but co-operating with it.

Underworld leaders coveted the Dutchman's fortune but he was eventually eliminated for political reasons. During the 1920s and early 1930s the criminals had prospered largely because of the extensive influence they wielded among corrupt (and not so corrupt) politicians.

Racketbusting

From about 1933, a reforming wind was blowing in the corridors of power. In place of notoriously corrupt Mayor Walker, New York got a campaigning, racketbusting mayor in Fiorello LaGuardia, and a new special prosecutor with a brief to clean up the rackets. This prosecutor was Thomas E. Dewey, an ambitious young lawyer who was later to bid twice for the presidency of the USA.

Dewey's first major target was

> " **You got a wife and kids, haven't you? You wouldn't like to see them in the river, would you?**
>
> LUCIANO'S MEN, to a New York politician "

Dutch Schultz. In 1933, a federal grand jury indicted Schultz on charges of income tax evasion on his bootlegging activities (it is a peculiarity of American law that taxes are cheerfully accepted on illegal business). The Dutchman had to go into hiding, and Luciano sent him to Albert Anastasia, a power in the docks in Brooklyn, who provided a safe bolthole.

Schultz eventually gave himself up, and in late 1934 a jury in Albany, a town well greased with Schultz's money, found him not guilty, a verdict with which the judge professed himself shocked. Back in New York, rumours quickly spread that Dewey intended to indict Schultz for his control of the restaurant protection racket, and even to charge him with murder and send him to the electric chair.

The Dutchman came excitedly to a meeting of the syndicate. Every morning, Schultz said, Dewey went into a drug store alone before being driven to his office. He could easily be killed there, and Schultz demanded that this should happen. But the syndicate dared not kill such a prominent man. Such a move would only increase the heat on themselves. The Dutchman stormed out, shouting that if they would not do it, he would carry out the murder himself.

Schultz had decreed no one's death but his own. A full meeting of the syndicate bosses voted Schultz's death. The contract on the Dutchman was given to Charlie 'The Bug' Workman, one of Luciano's most reliable bodyguards.

Contract fulfilled

On the evening of 23 October 1935, Schultz and three of his associates were in the Palace Chop House in Newark. Workman and a second killer entered and opened fire, killing Schultz's associates. Workman found Schultz in the men's room and shot him there. The Dutchman lingered on for a day, refusing to reveal, in true underworld fashion, who had killed him. This massacre was the underworld's bloodiest night since the St Valentine's Day Massacre in 1929.

Luciano and the syndicate inherited Schultz's share of the rackets. Their business was flourishing. The end of Prohibition in 1933 did not seriously halt the growth of crime. The Mob simply added trading in legal liquor to its illegal rackets. But the vogue for racketbusting was soon to claim a more illustrious victim than Schultz. The syndicate may have saved Dewey, but the prosecutor's next target was the 'king of crime' himself.

AP/Wide World

UPI/Bettmann Newsphotos

ILLEGAL GAMBLING

BACKGROUND

Gambling has always been the mainstay of US Mafia finances and, as most forms of gambling are illegal in most American states, the Mob has had rich pickings from a nation of dedicated gamblers. The Mafia controls, or has a large stake in, illicit poker games, the Numbers racket, bookmaking, sports betting and gambling casinos. Fruit machines were profitable in the 1930s and continue to be so today in places such as Las Vegas, a gambling Mecca started with Mob money. The Mafia's illegal profits have allowed it to move into legalized forms of gambling.

UPI/Bettmann Newsphotos

The scene at the Palace Chop House, in Newark, New Jersey, after the killing of Dutch Schultz and his three associates. Schultz, unlike many underworld leaders of the time, was a native New Yorker. His real name was Arthur Flegenheimer. His main criminal interests were bootlegging and the Numbers racket.

UPI/Bettmann Newsphotos

Gay Orlova (left), a Russian-born showgirl, was Lucky Luciano's mistress for a time. She went on to wed Edward Finn, a theatre usher, but the marriage was short-lived. In 1937, after a trip to Europe, immigration officials refused to allow her back into the USA.

THE NAKED CITY

A view down the East River (left), over the Manhattan and Brooklyn Bridges, to Wall Street, New York's financial district. The Fulton Fish Market, controlled by Joe 'Socks' Lanza, was also situated at the southern tip of New York's Manhattan Island.

Throughout the 20th century, gangs have divided up New York and each one has controlled a particular area. Gang leaders have come and gone and gang wars have altered the balance of power. Luciano grew up in this underworld and knew it well.

The five boroughs of New York City are mainly on three islands, connected by an intricate network of waterways. The city is one of the greatest concentrations of power and wealth in the world, and has long provided rich pickings for criminals to divide among themselves.

Early in the history of the Mafia a rough-and-ready territorial division was agreed. In 1919, when Ignazio 'the Wolf' Saietta went to jail, Johnny Torrio arranged a pact whereby Joe Masseria would control Little Italy and the Mulberry Bend area while Ciro Terranova would take uptown Manhattan.

Territory split

When the five New York crime 'families' were founded in the early 1930s, they also tended to specialize in certain areas. Three of the families – the Gambinos, Columbos and Bonannos – became centred in Brooklyn, where the authorities were more lenient towards crime. Lucky Luciano himself, however, viewed Brooklyn as foreign territory, and the Luciano (later Genovese) crime family operated largely in Manhattan itself.

Smaller areas were often the province of individual crime leaders. The Brooklyn waterfront was ruled for many years by Tough Tony Anastasio, brother of Albert

Anastasia, while Vito Genovese was boss of the Jersey docks. The Fulton Fish Market, which supplied the city with seafood, was the province of Joe 'Socks' Lanza from the 1920s to 1960s, despite his many terms in jail. When he died, the Market was taken over by the Genovese family.

The Mulberry Bend area (above), in Manhattan's Lower East Side, was where many newly arrived immigrants settled at the turn of the century. First, though, they had to pass through the immigration controls on Ellis Island (below), which also acted as a quarantine hospital.

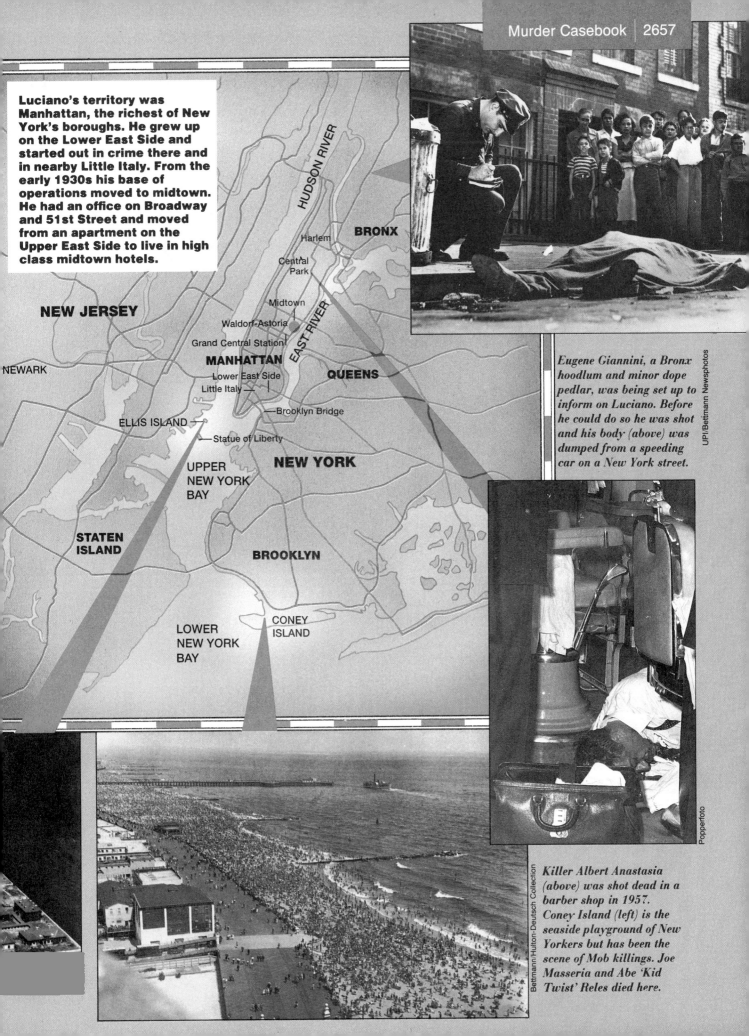

Luciano's territory was Manhattan, the richest of New York's boroughs. He grew up on the Lower East Side and started out in crime there and in nearby Little Italy. From the early 1930s his base of operations moved to midtown. He had an office on Broadway and 51st Street and moved from an apartment on the Upper East Side to live in high class midtown hotels.

HUDSON RIVER

BRONX

Harlem

Central Park

NEW JERSEY

Midtown

Waldorf-Astoria

Grand Central Station

EAST RIVER

MANHATTAN

NEWARK

QUEENS

Lower East Side

Little Italy

ELLIS ISLAND

Brooklyn Bridge

Statue of Liberty

NEW YORK

UPPER NEW YORK BAY

STATEN ISLAND

BROOKLYN

LOWER NEW YORK BAY

CONEY ISLAND

UPI/Bettmann Newsphotos

Eugene Giannini, a Bronx hoodlum and minor dope pedlar, was being set up to inform on Luciano. Before he could do so he was shot and his body (above) was dumped from a speeding car on a New York street.

Popperfoto

Bettmann/Hulton-Deutsch Collection

Killer Albert Anastasia (above) was shot dead in a barber shop in 1957. Coney Island (left) is the seaside playground of New Yorkers but has been the scene of Mob killings. Joe Masseria and Abe 'Kid Twist' Reles died here.

In Sing Sing

The special prosecutor had Luciano convicted. Efforts at racketbusting redoubled, aided by an informer who sent 13 hitmen to the electric chair. World War II gave Luciano his chance to earn a controversial reprieve.

The trial of Charles Lucania (a strange blending of Luciano's real and assumed names) and nine others on charges of compulsory prostitution opened at the New York State Supreme Court in downtown Manhattan, before Justice Philip J. McCook, on 13 May 1936. It may well be the case that prostitution was the only one of the major rackets in which Luciano was never actively involved. He denied it all his life. But then he also denied involvement in narcotics and there is ample evidence to link him with the drugs trade.

Hostile prosecution

In his pursuit of Luciano, Dewey, who prosecuted personally at the trial, used morally dubious methods which cast as much doubt retrospectively on himself as on Luciano. Dewey had arranged for special legislation to be rushed through early in 1936 so that multiple defendants could be tried on a 'joinder' system: firm evidence against certain defendants could cast guilt on others against whom the evidence was less clear.

Many of Dewey's witnessess were prostitutes, madams and small-time criminals hoping to win exemption from prosecution. Dewey often held them in solitary confinement, denying them the drugs on which they were dependent, setting impossibly high bails and exerting undue pressure on them to testify.

Even then, many of the witnesses

proved unsatisfactory in court. Frank Brown, the assistant manager of the Barbizon Plaza where Luciano had lived, declared on oath that he had never seen any of Luciano's alleged conspirators at the hotel. Dewey immediately had him declared a hostile witness. One of the prostitutes, Nancy Presser, declared that she had been Luciano's mistress (she also claimed he was impotent, thus raising a rumour which pursued Luciano throughout his life). Under questioning, however, she was unable to de-

Escorted by court officials, the jury of 12 business and professional men leaves court for lunch. The jury found each defendant guilty on all charges.

scribe his suite, or even whether he had a single or double bed.

None of this mattered. During cross-questioning, Dewey largely avoided the subject of prostitution, but he was able to catch Luciano out in lie after lie about the rackets. Judge McCook, a stern embodiment of moral outrage, made no secret of his hostility to Luciano and when, after three weeks of testimony, he was found guilty the judge sentenced him to the heaviest jail term ever given for compulsory prostitution – 30 to 50 years.

Luciano was taken briefly to Sing

Luciano (left) was extradited from the gambling spa of Hot Springs, Arkansas, to stand trial in New York's State Supreme Court in May 1936. His high-powered lawyers summed up with 13 hours of speeches for Luciano and his co-defendants, but to no avail. They were each found guilty on 62 counts. Justice McCook (right) passed a sentence intended to lock Luciano away for life.

JUN 36-FEB 46

18.6.36	Luciano sentenced
1937	Vito Genovese flees to Italy
24.8.39	Louis 'Lepke' Buchalter surrenders to FBI
12.11.41	Abe 'Kid Twist' Reles killed
9.2.42	*SS Normandie* sunk in Manhattan harbour
3.1.46	Luciano's release announced
9.2.46	Luciano deported

KEY DATES

UPI/Bettmann Newsphotos

PROSTITUTION RACKET

Luciano headed a Mafia racket that controlled New York's prostitutes.

Girls would phone bookers (pimps) on a Sunday to find out which house they would be working at that week. The 'house' would be a rented apartment run by a madam who solicited customers. When a house was raided by police, as happened every so often, the Mafia's bondsmen would pay the girls' bail and a disbarred lawyer would coach her in an alibi.

Eight out of ten who appeared in court were acquitted on their stories. Those who were sure to be convicted were told to disappear and their bail was forfeited. Of 170 cases investigated by Special Prosecutor Dewey's team, not one prostitute was sentenced to jail.

Luciano's enforcer, Little Davie Betillo, made sure that everyone, from lawyers and bondsmen to madams (such as Polly Adler, right) and whores, co-operated. Dewey estimated that the syndicate's profit in 1935, from 200 houses and 1,000 girls, was over $12 million.

IN CONTEXT

UPI/Bettmann Newsphotos

Sing Sing Prison in New York state (above) was one of the most notorious in the American system. Luciano spent the first part of his sentence there.

Sing prison, where he was diagnosed a syphilitic and drug addict (problems that were apparently taken care of during his jail years). He was then sent to Dannemora, known as 'Siberia' by the underworld. At first, he had to work in the laundry, but that did not last long. Soon, working in the library and holding court in the yard at exercise time, he was being treated as what he still was – king of the New York underworld.

Supreme boss

Although the trio of Frank Costello, Joe Adonis and Meyer Lansky effectively headed the syndicate during Luciano's absence, the evidence suggests that he was still regarded as supreme boss until well into the 1950s. Vito Genovese was ambitious to be crowned *capo di tutti capi*, but the rumour that he might be Dewey's next victim sent him fleeing to Mussolini's Italy in 1937.

The energies of the racket-busters were far from spent, and in 1937 they began a nationwide hunt for Louis 'Lepke' Buchalter. He was hidden by Albert Anastasia. By mid-1939 the syndicate decided that the authorities needed a sacrificial victim. Frank Costello persuaded Lepke that a deal had been worked out with FBI director J. Edgar Hoover. If Lepke surrendered he would face only minor charges.

Lepke insisted on surrendering to Hoover himself. There was, however, no deal. Within a month, Lepke was in a federal courtroom, charged with narcotics conspiracy.

Mafia informer

Worse was to come. Early in 1940, the former Murder Inc hitman Abe 'Kid Twist' Reles, in prison for murder, became the first major informer in Mafia history. His testimony sent a dozen minor hitmen to the electric chair, as well as Lepke, the former boss of Murder Inc.

Luciano, indirectly responsible for Lepke's fate, had always been willing to make that sacrifice, but he and other syndicate bosses became worried that the 'singing' of the canary Reles might endanger the lives of Murder Inc bosses Albert Anastasia

and Bugsy Siegel. Luciano gave the order for Reles to be killed. But the Kid was in 24-hour police custody on the sixth floor at the Half Moon Hotel in Coney Island, Brooklyn. Five guards were on duty in the early morning of 12 November 1941. Just before 7.00 a.m. an assistant manager heard a thud on an extension roof. When police later checked Reles's room, they found he was gone. The Kid's body could be seen 42 feet below, on the extension roof.

'It turned out the canary that could sing couldn't fly,' was the joke circulating among the relieved mobsters during the next few weeks. Luciano

never troubled to deny that he had ordered Reles's killing. It was odd, though, that a Mob hit could have been so easily achieved.

Implications

Towards the end of his life, Luciano claimed that the police were fully involved in the murder of Abe Reles. He implicated William O'Dwyer, Brooklyn district attorney at the time, who was directly responsible for Reles's custody, and who, in 1945, became a notoriously corrupt mayor of New York, in Mob pay.

America's involvement in World War II gave Luciano his chance for

Informer Abe Reles (right) was held under round-the-clock police guard. This did not prevent his death. Detectives (below) are seen examining his body at the Half Moon Hotel. District Attorney O'Dwyer had earlier prevented Reles from flying to the west coast to testify against Benny 'Bugsy' Siegel. The murder case against Siegel collapsed.

AP/Wide World. Inset: UPI/Bettmann Newsphotos

parole. By the end of February 1942, the US had lost 71 merchant ships to German submarines. American naval intelligence suspected that information was being passed to the enemy by German- or Italian-born Americans

Charles Haffenden, was aware that the Mob controlled all New York's piers and docks and it was decided to enlist the co-operation of the underworld.

The naval officers approached the

> **We have evidence of corruption of law-enforcement officers and connivance with criminal gangs in practically every city**
> KEFAUVER COMMITTEE, 1951

with connections on the waterfront. On 9 February, the great French ship *SS Normandie* was burnt while at her Manhattan berth and sabotage was suspected. A group at naval intelligence, led by Lieutenant Commander

relatively low-level fish market boss Joe 'Socks' Lanza, but quickly the answer came from the underworld that effective co-operation must come from the top, from Lucky Luciano. He was approached through his lawyer Moses Polakoff, and was at first reluctant to help without specific promises of release, but soon he was using his contacts to such effect that by the end of 1942 sabotage had almost vanished from the docks. During the later years of the war Luciano was allowed virtually unrestricted visits from his underworld friends.

Before the end of the war, Luciano had been moved from Dannemora to Great Meadow, the 'rest home' of the

SICILIAN INVASION

One of the factors in Luciano's 1946 release was said to have been the help he gave Allied forces in the 1943 invasion of Sicily. The wildest theories suggest that he was spirited from prison to Sicily to aid the war effort. However, since he left Sicily at the age of nine, he would have been of little practical use on the ground. More plausible is the suggestion that American Mafia contacts were able to liaise with Sicilian counterparts, who could provide guides and safe hideouts for Allied spies on the island.

New York prison system. On the day war ended, 7 May 1945, a petition for executive clemency was sent from Charles Lucania to his one-time prosecutor, Thomas E. Dewey, who was now governor of New York state. Dewey turned the matter over to the parole board, who were his appointees, and on 3 January 1946, Governor Dewey announced that Lucky Luciano was to be released, but only on condition that he be immediately deported for life to his native Sicily.

Controversy

The early release of Lucky Luciano, and Dewey's role in it, were the subject of controversy. In the early 1950s the affair was examined by a senate investigating committee, the Herlands Committee, which cleared Dewey of any blame. Nevertheless, their report was hushed by naval intelligence. The official version was that Luciano had been released as a reward for his wartime services.

This may be true, but many, including federal narcotics chief Harry J. Anslinger, were angry that such a persistent criminal had been freed,

UPI/Bettmann Newsphotos

The SS Normandie (above) burns at her Manhattan berth on the Hudson River. The former French luxury liner, once the fastest transatlantic passenger ship, was being converted into a troop ship.

and rumours have persisted that Luciano bought his freedom from Dewey. Towards the end of his life, Luciano claimed that he had amassed enough damaging material about Dewey, including evidence of misconduct at the 1936 trial, to blackmail the governor into setting him free.

Into exile

Lucky Luciano was put on board the *SS Laura Keene* on 8 February 1946, without being allowed to set foot in Manhattan. Newspapermen attempted to swarm aboard to interview him but Albert Anastasia's longshoremen barred their way with baling hooks. However, every major underworld figure and numerous New York politicians and dignitaries were allowed on board, and they took part in a splendid farewell party. Then, on the morning of 9 February, the ship set sail, taking Luciano into exile.

IN CONTEXT

THOMAS E. DEWEY

The first of the great American racketbusters and one of the great lost hopes of American politics, Thomas E. Dewey was the son of the editor of *The Owasso Times,* a small-town paper in Michigan. Dewey was a member of the American elite, whose family had been in America since 1634.

After graduating from Columbia University law school, he became a junior lawyer, then won fame in the mid-1930s as Special Prosecutor attacking organized crime. He progressed to become New York District Attorney, Governor of New York State, and made bids for the presidency as a Republican in 1944 and 1948.

But his behaviour over Luciano and others aroused suspicion. In 1951 he caused consternation by refusing to appear before a Congressional committee investigating organized crime.

In later life, he went into private law practice and became a close friend and adviser of President Richard Nixon. He died of heart failure in 1971, at the age of 68.

SMILING VILLAIN

Mafia boss, Lucky Luciano was an intelligent bully. He was also far-sighted, an entrepreneur who operated through a mixture of fear and charm.

Towards the end of Luciano's life, people sometimes remarked that he looked like a retired Italian dentist. The picture above may indeed give this impression. In reality, of course, he was a brutal killer and criminal mastermind, a man who boasted, 'I buried a hundred guys.'

Charles 'Lucky' Luciano had the prejudices, manners and habits of most of the Italians who came at the turn of the century to the Lower East Side. He would not automatically have stood out in a crowd as evil.

Early violence

There was another side to him, though. In his youth, particularly, Luciano had an enormous capacity for violence. It was this that drove him to become a criminal at a very early age. And he remained a criminal to the end. In his last years he was organizing the Italian end of the narcotics trade.

Luciano grew up in an Italian-American slum district. Like some of his friends, he saw violent crime as a way out of his situation. He practised for the Mafia at an early age, and he was anxious to kill for established mafiosi, 'to show that he was a man'.

Skilful leader

Luciano, however, was more intelligent than many mobsters. He had the imagination to take the disorganized gangs of the pre-Prohibition and Prohibition eras and turn them into a powerful national force. He started out as a violent young peasant but became a skilful, ruthless leader. To the end of his life he talked roughly, but the voice belied the brain.

And he had an important asset in ruling: charm. Throughout his life people

Luciano the street thug took on the role of successful, respectable businessman with ease. Both aspects of his character can be seen in these pictures, taken during his Italian exile. Having risen from the gutter in the 1920s he spent the rest of his life in an executive capacity, even during his years in jail.

were captivated by Luciano and could forget what he really was. When he was young, his Jewish employer, Max Goodman, was swayed by Luciano's charm and helped get him out of prison. Luciano's natural affinity with Jews showed that he had an ability to understand people, an ability that was beyond many suspicious Sicilians.

Luciano's charm won him the lifelong friendship of Meyer Lanksy, who saw that he was well supplied by the Mob even in exile. In ex-

ile, too, his charming manners helped his mistress, Igea Lissoni, to love a man she knew to be a murderous gangster.

Wrong path

Towards the end of his life, Luciano said that if he had his time again he would devote the energies he had devoted to crime to legitimate business. He might have made a fortune in legitimate business. But it is a revelation of what he really was that from first to last Luciano chose crime.

Going Home

Luciano's exile in Italy was broken only by a Mafia meeting in Cuba. Nevertheless, he kept control of the US Mafia and set up an international drugs ring. He avoided the police, fell in love and died a natural death.

On arrival at Genoa, Italy, Luciano was deported to live at his home town of Lercara Friddi in Sicily, where he was treated as a local boy made good. This self-made *milionario* soon gained permission to live in Palermo, where he made contact with Calogero 'Don Calo' Vizzini, the supreme Mafia boss in Sicily. Before long, Luciano persuaded the slightly old-fashioned Vizzini that the future lay in narcotics in a big way. The two men began laying the foundations of a business which would import $150 million worth of heroin into the USA in the ten years of the 1950s.

But Luciano did not intend to be bound by Italy for long. His ultimate aim was to return to the United States. In late September 1946, Luciano

Under pressure from the US, Luciano (top) was deported from Cuba. He was met by Italian police on arrival at Genoa.

Tooham

KEY DATES

1946-1969

22.12.46	Havana conference begins
20.6.47	Bugsy Siegel killed
20.9.52	Eugene Giannini killed
1957	Frank Costello retires as Mafia head
27.9.58	Igea Lissoni dies
1959	Vito Genovese imprisoned
1959	Luciano has heart attack
26.1.62	Luciano dies at Naples Airport
29.1.62	Requiem mass, Naples
7.2.62	Luciano buried in New York
1969	Genovese dies in prison

UPI/Bettmann Newsphotos

MEYER LANSKY

IN CONTEXT

Meyer Lansky was one of the most ingenious and creative men to devote themselves to crime in America in the 20th century. He was born of Jewish parents in Russian Poland in 1902 and arrived in the US at the age of nine.

In his youth, when he ran the Bugs and Meyer gang with his friend Bugsy Siegel, the diminutive Lansky was a killer. He always remained ruthless, but his style became quieter and more relaxed. Known as 'The Brain', he was the man who took the Mob into big business and masterminded the laundering of illegal money. The extensive gambling operations of the Mafia in pre-Castro Cuba were largely his work.

AP/Wide World

The Hotel Nacional (above) in Havana, Cuba, was the scene of a shoot-out during a 1933 coup that brought Batista to power. Luciano stayed there in 1946 and met US Mafia bosses.

obtained two Italian passports in the name of Salvatore Lucania. In late October, he checked in to the Hotel Nacional in Havana, Cuba, only 90 miles from the United States. Cuba, under the corrupt dictatorship of Fulgencio Batista, had long been a centre of Mob activities, particularly in gambling. Meyer Lansky had arranged the booking, and he was also arranging another major conference of the American underworld. This was

> ## Luciano was nothing but a pimp and a dope pedlar which, ironically, are the two things no gangster wants to be considered
> CHARLES SIRAGUSA

scheduled to begin on 22 December and every major leader would be present.

At the conference, Luciano was able to beat off a challenge to his leadership from Vito Genovese, who had now returned to the United States. But the conference was chiefly notable for the decision, made in a private meeting between Luciano and the other major leaders, to kill Bugsy Siegel, one of Luciano's oldest friends and someone he had known since childhood.

From the late 1930s, Siegel had been taking care of the Outfit's activities on the west coast, where he concentrated largely on gambling.

Siegel had picked on what was then a small town, Las Vegas, and in the immediate post-war years he was building a massive hotel there called the Flamingo. The syndicate leaders, however, were concerned that Siegel was diverting too much of their money into this enterprise. He was also struggling with other underworld leaders for control of the wire service which supplied bookies with racetrack information. The Havana meeting decided that Siegel had to go, and even Meyer Lansky, who had so admired the tall, handsome Siegel when they were the leaders of the 'Bugs and Meyer' gang, did not dissent.

On the evening of 20 June 1947, Siegel was relaxing in the Beverly Hills home of his mistress Virginia Hill, the notorious 'bag lady' (courier)

Virginia Hill (above), was known as a courier for the Mob. She was reputed to have kept Luciano supplied with money during his years in Italy.

of the Mob. She was in Europe at the time. Suddenly a fusillade from an army carbine tore through the window and into Siegel's face and body. His ribs and vertebrae were cracked, his lungs blown out, and his right eye was later discovered on the floor 15 feet away. The friend who was sitting with him, Allen Smiley, was unharmed but Siegel lay dead.

Avoiding prosecution

Harry Anslinger of the Federal Bureau of Narcotics got wind that Luciano was in Cuba and had him deported. But even back in exile in Italy, Luciano still sometimes felt the need to order killings in the United States. Early in 1951 federal narcotics chief Anslinger sent a new undercover agent to Italy. He was Charles Siragusa, an Italian-American who

IGEA LISSONI

BACKGROUND

Igea Lissoni was a beautiful and well-educated girl from Milan. She trained to be a ballet dancer at La Scala Opera, but gave it up for nightclub performing when she discovered she did not have enough talent to be a top ballerina.

She met Luciano in 1947 when she was dancing at a club in Rome. He courted her with old-fashioned persistence and, although she was initially horrified by his gangster reputation, she became his mistress.

They spent a happy decade together and, with her encouragement, Luciano started reading books, including Shakespeare. She could not persuade him to accompany her to the ballet, however. He thought it was simply a gang of effeminate men dressed up in tights!

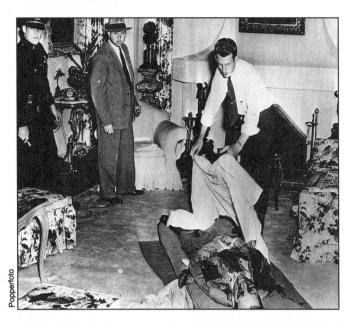

Popperfoto

Bugsy Siegel was 42 when he was shot dead by Mafia hitmen in the home (left) of his mistress, Virginia Hill. Siegel was hit by five of the nine bullets fired. A man with film-star good looks, he had become a minor celebrity with movie people in Hollywood, and counted screen actor George Raft as a close friend.

had grown up in the Bronx and learnt to hate the rackets there, and he made dedicated efforts to indict Luciano for drug smuggling. Siragusa was able to persuade a minor American hoodlum, Eugene Giannini, a dope pedlar sent to Italy from the USA by Vito Genovese, to inform on Luciano while in custody.

The Italian police deported Giannini and, rather foolishly perhaps, he returned to the United States in April 1952. He was there five months. Luciano sent word to Genovese about the informant, and on 20 September 1952, Joe Valachi and two other men shot Giannini on an East Harlem Street.

Luciano's life in Italy in the 1950s was quite a pleasant one. Although

THE HEARINGS

In 1950 and 1951 the existence of a Mafia was first revealed to millions of Americans by the Senate Committee to Investigate Organized Crime. Chaired by Democrat senator Estes Kefauver (right), it was popularly called 'the Kefauver Hearings.' The committee toured major US cities, hearing testimony from mobsters and law-enforcement officials.

The hearings were televised, and the previously unknown Senator Kefauver became something of a national hero. One letter he received read, 'I am a small time racketeer. Don't know nothing but think you are a swell guy.'

The hearings, however, often generated more amusement than enlightenment. The nation was fascinated by the hand dance of Frank Costello – the ageing mobster had forbidden his face to be shown. Bag-lady Virginia Hill said on oath that she hoped an atom bomb fell on the court.

But the hearings did have some concrete effects. Frank Costello's power was broken and Joe Adonis was deported.

Most talkative (although incoherent) of the mobsters was Willie Moretti who was suffering from syphilitic deterioration. One of the committee members said he had found Moretti's testimony 'rather refreshing'. The Mob had Moretti killed. As one commentator remarked, 'Everyone liked Willie Moretti. They just liked him better dead.'

IN CONTEXT

AP/Wide World

Italian and American police knew him to be one of the major figures behind the growing narcotics trade to the States, there was little they could do to nail him. Restrictions were often placed on his ability to travel, and, in 1949, he was briefly held in jail, but police lacked the hard evidence to convict him.

In 1955, when Siragusa became the European director of the United States Bureau of Narcotics, Luciano was barred from leaving his house between dusk and dawn and from travelling more than 16 miles outside Naples, where he now lived. Despite this, he was able to talk about his troubles to reporters and visitors, and he became quite a tourist attraction on the Naples waterfront. He opened a couple of legitimate businesses, one selling electrical goods and the other medical equipment, and the Mob kept

> **I'm no millionaire or institution, but there's a lot of poor people in Naples who need help. I do what I can**
> LUCKY LUCIANO

him supplied with money through its courier Virginia Hill.

Luciano also found love. From the late 1940s, he was closely involved with the beautiful and cultured Igea Lissoni, who was perhaps the only great love of his life. They never married, however, nor did they have children. In 1958, Igea died tragically of cancer at the early age of 37. After that, Luciano lived until his death with a young Neapolitan girl, Adriana Rizzo.

New boss

Luciano retained control over the affairs of the Mafia in America, although by the late 1950s his grip on it had almost failed. Acting head of the syndicate until 1957 was Frank Costello, but a near-successful attempt on his life frightened him into retirement. Vito Genovese then made his bid to be boss of all bosses, and was successful in this. In 1959, however, a non-Mafia informer, with the

unlikely name of Nelson Cantellops, landed him in prison for narcotics conspiracy, and he died there ten years later. It is believed that Luciano arranged for Genovese, once his friend and now his enemy, to be informed upon and arrested.

End of the story

Luciano's end was a strange one. In 1959 he had a major heart attack but recovered. About the same time, he met a Hollywood film producer, Barnet Glassman, and agreed to let him produce a film to be called *The Lucky Luciano Story*. Glassman employed an assistant, Martin Gosch, to write the script.

In January 1962 Luciano suddenly summoned Gosch, who was in Madrid at the time, to see him in Naples. Gosch's version of this is that the Mob in America had forbidden the filming of Luciano's life. Biographer Tony Scaduto, however, claims that Luciano was angry with Gosch about the script and planned to discuss it with him.

Luciano went to Naples' Capodichini Airport on 26 January 1962 to meet Gosch's plane. Narcotics police had raided Luciano's flat the previous day, apparently because a phone call from Gosch about a 'script' had made them think they were dealing with a drugs carrier. Naples police official Cesare Resta watched Luciano at the airport, and there were apparently plans to take him in.

AP/Wide World

Martin Gosch (above) worked with Luciano on a script for an intended film of Luciano's life. The film was never made.

Charles Siragusa (below) was the US narcotics agent who attempted to curtail the international drug smuggling ring which Luciano set up.

UPI/Bettmann Newsphotos

Both Photos Popperfoto

Luciano collapsed and died from a heart attack at Naples' Capodichini Airport on 26 January 1962. The Mafia boss had been on his way out of the airport with scriptwriter Martin Gosch. Although airport workers rushed to help the prostrate body (left), Luciano died almost immediately. He was 64 years old. Three days later, mourners followed his elaborate hearse through the streets of Naples to a requiem mass. Among them was Luciano's brother, Bartolo Lucania, (centre below, in a light overcoat and dark glasses).

Gosch's plane arrived soon after 5.00 p.m., and Luciano met him at the arrivals exit. So many versions exist of what they said to each other that it is impossible to say which is the correct one. What is certain is that as they were walking towards the exit, Luciano collapsed from a massive heart attack and died almost immediately.

Stylish send-off

Three days later the requiem mass was held at Holy Trinity Church in Naples. Old friend Joe Adonis, also deported to Italy, got permission from police to attend the funeral. In true old gangster style, Adonis produced a massive floral tribute with the words, 'So long, Pal'.

It had been Luciano's wish that his remains be buried at the family vault he had purchased in 1935 at St John's Cemetery, Middle Village, Queens, where his father, mother, an aunt and an uncle were already lying. In death, his wish to return to the US was granted, and Luciano was interred there on 7 February 1962.

AFTERMATH

had been killed. Two men, who have remained unidentified, burst in and fired ten bullets, killing Anastasia. Leadership of his crime family passed to Carlo Gambino.

■ Vito Genovese fled the USA in 1937 on a murder charge. He ingratiated himself with the Italian dictator Mussolini, becoming chief drugs supplier to Count Ciano, an addict who was Mussolini's son-in-law and foreign minister. Despite this, Genovese found no difficulty in attaching himself to the Allied forces when Italy fell to them. After his return to the USA, Genovese ordered the killing of Albert Anastasia and ordered the abortive hit on Frank Costello to win himself supreme power in 1957. He was sent to prison in 1959 and died there in 1969. Like Lucky Luciano, he was buried at St John's Cemetery, Queens, a favourite resting place of mobsters.

■ Meyer Lansky, who married twice, was a patriotic family American. He took im-

mense pride in his son becoming an officer at West Point military academy, and was a fervent supporter of America's involvement in the Vietnam War. He was a criminal multi-millionaire, but courted anonymity with such success that he avoided trouble with the law until almost the end of his life. In the 1970s, he had to move to Israel for a while when indicted by a federal grand jury. He returned to the US and died in 1983, the last survivor of a legendary generation of mobsters.

■ *The Godfather*, released in 1972, was the most successful American film since *Gone With The Wind.* The Mafia boss, Don Vito Corleone, who was played by Robert De Niro and (as an old man) by Marlon Brando, is thought to have been based on Carlo Gambino. He was a mild-mannered but ruthless Mafia leader whose career lasted from the 1930s to the 1970s. Corleone is the name of a town in Sicily.

■ Al Capone was released from Atlanta's Federal Jail and later Alcatraz in 1939. He had served eight years of an 11 year prison sentence for tax evasion. Capone retired to his large Palm Island estate in Florida where he enjoyed a quiet and sedate lifestyle. He was also suffering from paresis, a brain wasting disease, developed from an early case of syphilis. For the next eight years he kept out of the public eye. After outlasting four Chiefs of Police, two Municipal Administrations, three US District Attorneys and a regiment of Federal prohibition agents, Al Capone finally died peacefully in bed, in January 1947, aged 52.

■ Albert Anastasia served as a technical sergeant instructing GIs during World War II. He went on to murder his way to overlordship of the Mangano crime family in 1951. On 25 October 1957, Anastasia was sitting in a barber's chair in Manhattan's Park Sheraton Hotel, the hotel where Arnold Rothstein

Frank Costello (above) was nicknamed 'The Prime Minister'. He, along with Joe Adonis and Meyer Lansky, took charge of the New York Mafia when Luciano was jailed and continued to run it when Luciano was deported. In a real sense Costello served as a prime minister to the unquestioned king of American crime. Costello is seen above at the 1951 Kefauver Hearings, where he refused to answer questions. Marlon Brando (right) in a scene from The Godfather, *a film based around the Mafia.*

FOR MONTHS throughout 1890—the year in which the Mafia first outraged New Orleans—the city's chief of police, David Hennessey, had gathered evidence against the organization which had established a stranglehold on the waterfront and docks. The busy Louisiana port was one of the most vital links with the Latin American fruit trade—which was rapidly growing in prosperity and importance.

However, no banana boat could unload its cargo until "dues" had been paid to the Matranga brothers, Antonio and Carlo, from Palermo, Sicily. Anyone—owner or worker—who refused to "do business" with the Matrangas was liable to have his throat cut, be shot outside his home, or else beaten half to death and then thrown into one of the canals. It was this reign of bloodshed and terror that Hennessey had sworn to end.

Due to threats made to himself and his staff, his was practically a one-man campaign. Ignoring the threats, and contemptuously rejecting the bribes that went before or after them, he methodically built up his dossier. A snippet of information here, a tidbit of gossip there, a word from an informer, a tip from a mem-

WATERFRONT WARFARE . . . Police chief David Hennessey (right) set out to end Mafia operations in New Orleans docks (below). His reward was a savage death.

DAVID HENNESSEY

ber of a rival gang. This was how he gathered enough facts, enough evidence to put a case before a grand jury. And that was what he shortly intended to do on the evening that he left police headquarters and began to walk through the darkened streets to his home.

Suddenly, four men came out of the misty night and aimed shotguns at him.

They opened fire at point-blank range, riddling his body with pellets. Even though mortally wounded, Hennessey dragged out his service revolver from where he lay on the sidewalk. Propping himself up on one arm, he fired at his attackers until they melted into the blackness and he had no bullets left. Then, using the last of his strength, he dragged himself to the stoop of a nearby house—where he was discovered by one of his own detectives. The police chief, close to death, managed to say one word, "Dagoes".

Nineteen Sicilians were tried for the murder of David Hennessey, 60 witnesses were persuaded to give evidence against the Mafia members, and it was then that the organization moved in armed with money in one hand and a gun in the other. The jurors were so intimidated that they acquitted 16 of the defendants, and could come to no decision about the other three.

Infuriated by the verdicts, a mob of New Orleans citizens stormed the jail in which the accused were still being held. Two of the Mafia men were hanged from lamp posts outside the prison, and 9 more were lined up against a wall and shot. Shortly before that the mayor, Joseph A. Shakespeare, told the city: "The Sicilians who come here must become American citizens and obey the law of the land, or else there is no place for them in our country."

EXPLOSIONS rock the night air, ships disappear in mid ocean, mysterious fires spread death and havoc in factories and warehouses. It is all the work of a few relentless men bent on destruction . . .

INDUSTRIAL TERROR BOMBERS

FRIENDLY FARMER Harry Orchard tends his chickens at Idaho State Prison Farm. But back in 1905 this smiling figure blew up the ex-governor of the state (above inset). His attempt to implicate union leaders was foiled by great criminal lawyer Clarence Darrow (right).

IT WAS nearly noon on November 21, 1903, and the superintendent of the Vindicator silver mine, Cripple Creek, Colorado, set out on a routine check of the mine with his shift boss. They walked cautiously; for the past three months there had been constant trouble at the mine; the miners were on strike, the National Guard had been called in, and the night watchman had seen shadowy figures wandering around.

The two men reached the sixth level, and Charles McCormick gripped a handrail to steady himself. The sound of a revolver shot made them both fling themselves backwards; then there was a tremendous roar, and the mine collapsed around them, killing them both. Later, in the wreckage, investigators found the remains of a twisted revolver. Its trigger had been attached to the handrail with a fishing line, so that when anyone grasped the shaky rail, a bullet was fired into a bundle of dynamite sticks.

Union clash

The Cripple Creek mine explosion was one of the first acts of industrial sabotage in American history. But in those days it was not known as sabotage. The word only came into general use after a French railway strike of 1912, when railwaymen cut the shoes (or "sabots") of the railway lines to wreck trains. But sabotage, or industrial wrecking, had been preached by trade union organizations for more than 50 years; the first recorded instance of it occurred when Sheffield workers destroyed the tools of blacklegs (strike-breakers) in the 1860's.

That Cripple Creek mine explosion was not quite the first piece of industrial sabotage in American history. As early as 1892, there had been a clash between union and non-union miners at the Frisco mine at Gem, Idaho. Fifteen men died in the fight; then the strikers blew up the mine. Again, in 1899, a gang from Burke, Idaho, blew up the Bunker-Hill-Sullivan mine at Wardner, Idaho. These cases were not, perhaps, "sabotage" in the modern sense. But an explosion that occurred soon after the Cripple Creek incident *was*. On June 6, 1904, 26 non-union men from a mine at Independence, Colorado, were standing on the platform at a train depot after finishing their day's work. A sudden explosion turned the depot into matchwood, killing 14 of the men and seriously injuring the rest—some were crippled for life.

On November 17, 1904, Fred Bradley, ex-manager of the Bunker-Hill-Sullivan mine walked into the hall of his San Francisco home and lit a cigar; the next moment a discharge blew him straight out of the door. Although seriously injured, he recovered, and the San Francisco gas company subsequently paid him nearly $11,000 in damages, assuming the explosion to be due to a faulty gas main.

On December 30, 1905, Frank Steunenburg, ex-governor of Idaho, opened his garden gate, and was hurled into the air by a blast of dynamite. His wife rushed out to find the snow stained with blood, and her husband unrecognizable – and dying. The police acted quickly. All roads out of the city were closed, and the hotels were searched. They were in luck; the proprietor of the Saratoga Hotel thought that one of his guests had been acting suspiciously; when the police called the next day, the man was still there. In his room, the police found potassium chlorate, and other explosive ingredients. He was a small, cheerful-looking Irishman with a round, red face, and he gave his name as Harry Orchard. Many people at the time recorded the impression that he didn't *want* to get away – that he sought out the notoriety and publicity that he felt were his due. And he got them.

Planted bomb

He confessed to a whole series of crimes. He had personally lighted the fuse that blew up the Bunker-Hill-Sullivan mine; he had planted the dynamite and revolver in the Cripple Creek mine; he had planted the bomb that blew up the railway station at Independence; he had blown up Governor Steunenburg, *and* Fred Bradley. The explosion that blew Bradley out of his own front door was not gas; it was pure coincidence that it took place as he lit a cigar.

Having got himself arrested, Harry Orchard – whose real name was Albert Horsley – proceeded to wriggle his neck out of the hangman's noose. The first thing he did was to implicate several leaders of the Western Federation of Miners Union, including William Haywood, George Pettibone, and Charles Moyer. He then had a religious "revelation", and declared himself to be a reformed man who had seen the light. He told reporters smugly that he had believed he was engaged in a class war, but that since God had enlightened him, he realized he had only been seeking revenge. His plan worked; he was sentenced to life imprisonment, and subsequently became a Seventh Day Adventist and a leading preacher in the penitentiary.

But if Orchard's conversion was unworthy of a revolutionary, his methods were an inspiration to labour saboteurs the world over. At the Independence railroad depot, a hundred pounds of dynamite had been placed under the floor. Detonating caps were placed on the dynamite. Above them, attached to a small wheel, was a bottle of sulphuric acid. A long wire fixed to the wheel meant that the acid could be tilted on to the caps

International News

BLACK TOM promontory blazes furiously after violent explosions set off by saboteurs in 1916. Damage was estimated at $22,000,000.

at any time. Orchard was several hundred yards away when he tugged the wire that sent the station sky high.

He had got into Fred Bradley's home by becoming the lover of one of his servant girls. He used the same device – sulphuric acid on a kind of windlass. This time, however, the wire was attached to the door, so that the dynamite would explode when the door was opened. The same dynamite and acid-bottle device was used to blow up Mr. Frank Steunenburg.

There is one interesting point about Orchard's long confession. For all its pious expressions of repentance for his crimes, it is obvious that he enjoyed every minute of his strange manhunts. He had discovered a new sport that combined the adult's love of hunting with the child's delight in causing loud bangs. It is a characteristic that appears in many saboteurs.

Labour hero

In spite of Orchard's confessions, the accused Union leaders managed to escape largely due to the brilliant efforts of the great advocate, Clarence Darrow. Darrow became the hero of the American labour movement, and Pettibone, Moyer and the rest were regarded as near-martyrs. In retrospect, it seems more than

likely that the Union leaders *were* accessories. They were fortunate in that America's greatest criminal lawyer chose to defend them.

America suddenly discovered the full meaning of sabotage in World War I. The United States had a high population of immigrant Germans, many of them American citizens. Even before the United States entered the war, in April 1917, it was supplying England with arms and food. And then the explosions began. It was on a hot June evening in 1916 that a guard in the great freight yards of Black Tom – the promontory of New Jersey that faces New York City – was startled to see a fire burning under a railroad wagon loaded with munitions. Then he saw another fire a hundred yards away. He rang the fire alarm, but a quarter of an hour later tremendous explosions sent a column of smoke and fire into the air.

The whole freight yard, full of munitions for the Allies, went off like a giant bomb. The concussion was enough to have destroyed the skyscrapers of Wall Street, but the force of the blast went upwards; only two adults and a child were killed. A landlady subsequently reported that her lodger, a Hungarian named Michael Kristoff, had been pacing his room all night after the explosion groaning "What have I done?" An American agent actually got an admission of guilt out of Kristoff; then Kristoff disappeared. Ironically, he had been arrested for a civil offence, and put in jail, where

Brown Brothers

UPI

he stayed for the duration of the war.

On the other side of the country, in San Francisco, a German reported to the authorities that he had heard of a plot to blow up the Mare Island Navy Yard. Before the authorities could act, the yard erupted in flames and suffered explosions as violent as those at Black Tom. This time 16 children were among the dead.

The solution of the Mare Island explosion came by chance, after the outbreak of war in 1917. Although Mexico was neutral, there was much anti-Americanism there, and the Mexican police made no attempt to harass Germans who were obviously spies. Washington persuaded Paul Altendorf, a colonel in the Mexican army, to act as a counter-spy. In Mexico City bars, Altendorf made the acquaintance of Kurt Jahnke, who was suspected of being an enemy agent. Jahnke was a heavy drinker. One day, in a confiding mood, he told Altendorf that he was the patriotic citizen who had reported the plot to blow up Mare Island to the authorities – and also the man who had-then blown it up. He had reported it because he knew that he would then be

the last person to be suspected of the explosion.

Jahnke was an explosives expert, who worked in combination with Lothar Witzke, another of Germany's most skilled saboteurs. Altendorf, pretending to be as anti-American as Jahnke, offered his aid in future projects. Jahnke said that Witzke needed help finding his way back across the Mexican border into the United States. Altendorf said that he knew the country intimately and would be glad to help. The consequence was that when Witzke arrived in Nogales, Arizona, he found American Secret Service men waiting to arrest him. He was subsequently sentenced to death, but reprieved and later allowed to return to Germany.

Beautiful spy

The end of the Witzke-Jahnke team was one of the triumphs that helped to put a stop to sabotage in World War I; the other was the capture of the beautiful German spy, Maria von Kretschman. This was due to a fortunate accident: a courier put two letters into the wrong envelopes. On the advice of British Intelligence,

SPY TRAPPER Paul Altendorf (right) in Mexican army uniform broke up the deadly team of Lothar Witzke (above top) and Kurt Jahnke (centre). Background picture shows Mare Island Navy Yard, one of Jahnke's "successes".

American agents were already watching an address on Long Island. A letter was duly intercepted, and the agents were puzzled. The envelope was addressed to a man – one of the German agents they were on the lookout for – but the letter inside was to a woman.

Chemical technicians tested the letter, and found another letter on the back, written in invisible ink. It was about the blowing up of munitions factories and mines. With excitement, the agents realized they had stumbled on a key figure in the sabotage network. But who was she? They traced the courier who had sent the letter – he had put his return address on the envelope – a sailors' lodging-house – but that didn't help much.

The man was simply a go-between who had agreed to post the two letters when

agents managed to find another cache of unopened "Victorica" letters at another *poste restante* address; but again the trail led nowhere. All they proved was that Victorica *was* involved in the series of explosions that were rocking American factories and dockyards every other week. The Secret Service then deployed dozens of agents to watch every person mentioned in the letters. They maintained their surveillance for weeks, and no one did anything suspicious. One weary agent reported to his chief that the young sister of one of the suspects seemed to be very religious — she never missed going to church. His chief looked up sharply. "In that case, follow her, you fool!"

Prayed briefly

His intuition proved to be correct. The next day, the agent saw the young girl kneel down in St. Patrick's Cathedral in Fifth Avenue, and place a newspaper on the seat; when she left, the newspaper was still there. Another man moved into the pew, prayed briefly, and left carrying the newspaper. The man went to a Long Island hotel, the Nassau, sat in the lounge for a few minutes. Then he walked out, leaving the newspaper behind. A tall, beautiful blonde woman in her thirties then sat down and casually picked it up.

A few days later, she was under arrest, the elusive Madame Victorica — whose real name was Maria von Kretschman. Under interrogation, she confessed — and told the agents how she had used religion to aid her activities as a key saboteur. She persuaded Catholic priests to help her in ordering religious statuettes from Zürich, in Switzerland. When the statuettes arrived, they would be full of chemicals vital to the detonating of explosives. The nervous strain had been telling on her; now that she was arrested, she cracked. (She died, a drug addict, a few years later.) With her capture, and the break-up of the Jahnke-Witzke partnership, the United States had eliminated the sabotage ring that had been causing so much damage.

The damage might have been worse if one of Germany's master spies — and saboteurs — had not been hamstrung by jealousy from bureaucrats at home. Franz Rintelen von Kleist — usually known simply as Von Rintelen — got into the United States on a Swiss passport in the month America declared war. His speciality was sabotage.

A German-American, Dr. Schlee, had invented a new incendiary device, no bigger than a fountain pen. It was divided in half by a thin copper wall. One half contained picric acid, the other half, sulphuric acid. When the sulphuric acid ate through the copper, a brilliant, hot flame shot out of the device. It was called a Thermit pencil. Von Rintelen contacted Schlee, arranged for the manufacture of hundreds of Thermit pencils, and passed them on to Irish dock workers who hated the British — and who dropped them into cracks on munition ships about to depart for England.

Soon there were fires at sea, and the British realized that a new master saboteur was at work. Another German inventor named Fay produced a kind of bomb that would explode as the rudder of a ship moved from side to side; it was attached by a magnet, like a modern limpet mine. The mysterious fires at sea were then supplemented by mysterious explosions that destroyed the ship's rudder.

Von Rintelen's brilliance was his own undoing. Congratulatory messages came from high sources in the Fatherland, and passed through the Washington Embassy. Jealousies and resentments flared. To Von Rintelen's alarm, the men who should have been protecting him began to commit indiscretions; one day, he actually received a letter addressed to him with his correct name (he was under an alias, naturally) and military title. As American agents closed in, he slipped on board a ship. All might have been well; but the ship stopped at Southampton. Although his passport said he was a Swiss citizen, Von Rintelen was questioned. Suddenly, the interrogator tried an old trick; he yelled in German: "Salute" — and Von Rintelen's heels automatically clicked together.

Greatest saboteur

Even then, he succeeded in escaping from custody, and was finally captured in Leicester. The great British spy chief, Admiral "Blinker" Hall, took advantage of his resentment about the German Embassy to get him to cooperate with British Intelligence. The man who could have been Germany's top saboteur of World War I was turned into a traitor by the petty envy and jealousy of his superiors.

The greatest saboteur of all time was also a German, although he devoted his life to working for Soviet Russia. Ernst Friedrich Wollweber was born in 1898, the son of a Hamburg miner. He was short, chunky, ugly, and driven by immense energy; later in life, he became an obese dwarf. It may have been some desire to compensate for his unattractive appearance that turned Wollweber into a revolutionary. In 1917, he joined the German navy; inspired by the Russian Revolution, he preached Socialism below decks. It was Wollweber's propaganda that helped stir the German fleet to mutiny in November 1918, and he personally hauled up the Red Flag on the

he landed in New York. It was he who had removed the letters from their grubby old envelopes, and in re-addressing them, put them back in the wrong envelopes. He could even recall the address on the other envelope — but again the agents were frustrated. An old lady who lived there said she sometimes received letters for someone else, but she couldn't give any more information — except that she had once seen the name "Victorica" on one of them.

That didn't seem much to go on. The

cruiser *Heligoland* at the entrance to the Kiel Canal – the signal for the revolt.

In Bremen, Wollweber led rioters on the Oslebhausen prison, and saw the prisoners set free. He hoped for a swift Communist triumph in Germany – but he was disappointed. Even in defeat, Germany was not ready for revolution. The Weimar Republic was formed in 1919 and Wollweber responded by leading another mutiny on board ship, and took the vessel to Murmansk, as a present for the Soviet regime. As a reward for this, he was appointed by Lenin as chairman of the International Seamen's Union. He sailed round the world, acting as an emissary of Communism in China, Japan, Italy, and the United States.

Undismayed

The Communists were shocked by the ease with which Hitler destroyed the German Communist Party when he came to power in 1933. But Wollweber was typically undismayed. He chose Copenhagen as his headquarters, and settled down to a career as a master saboteur. Ships left Denmark loaded with supplies for the Fascists in the Spanish Civil War. Wollweber's agents mixed TNT with the coal, and many of the ships failed to reach Spanish ports, or had their cargoes destroyed by fire.

One of Wollweber's great triumphs was the destruction of the German troopship *Marion*, which left Denmark for Norway in 1940. A shattering explosion sank the ship, and badly burned corpses floated ashore for weeks afterwards – 4000 of them. When the Nazis invaded Denmark, Wollweber moved to Sweden. Although he was promptly arrested, he had already succeeded in organizing a sabotage ring there. His agent, Jacob Liebersohn, had

MUTINEERS MARCH through the streets of Kiel in November 1918. Their rising was carefully planned by master saboteur Wollweber (inset) as East German Security Minister.

MASTER SPY Von Rintelen was a victim of jealousy. His German superiors destroyed his cover – so he changed sides . . .

recruited two young waitresses, Erika Möller and Gunhild Ahman. They were ideal agents; no one suspected two women. They were responsible for the explosion that destroyed part of the freight yards at Krylbo, in central Sweden, on July 19, 1941 – and detonated truckloads of German shells. There were many more fires and explosions before the counter-espionage branch of the Swedish Statspolisen arrested the two women and their accomplices, and sent them to prison.

The Swedes kept Wollweber in jail until the end of the war, in spite of Nazi demands that he be handed over. As soon as it was clear that the Nazis were losing the war, however, they allowed Wollweber to go to Moscow. There, he was treated as a Soviet hero, and entered Berlin not far behind Marshal Zhukov. Declining important political appointments, he went back to organizing an East German spy ring. He enjoyed undercover work. He may also have felt that a

public appointment would restrict his sex life – for he was known as an insatiable satyr.

Again, there were explosions on British and American ships – the fire on the *Queen Elizabeth* in 1953 was almost certainly Wollweber's work. But that was one of his last achievements in sabotage; in that year, he was appointed Minister of State Security in East Germany. There *was* a point in 1961 when it looked as if Wollweber's luck was at last running out; after a clash with Walter Ulbricht, the Secretary of the East German Communist Party ordered Wollweber's arrest. Wollweber contacted Moscow, and a telegram arrived: "Let Wollweber alone, he is a friend of mine". It was signed "Krushchev". So Wollweber died a natural death after all, in 1962.

It is the fate of the saboteur to live in an emotional no man's land, with no place that he can openly call his own. His existence – and psychological condition – is one of constant uncertainty, fear, and suspicion. He is like a man who has betrayed his wife *and* the mistress whom he has set in her place. He is his own worst enemy.

THE ANARCHISTS

Were Nicola Sacco
and Bartolomeo Vanzetti,
two radical Italian
immigrants, really
executed for their
political beliefs.
Or did they commit
robbery and murder . . ?

IMMORTALIZED . . . Ben Shahn's
famous painting reminds the world of
the deaths of Italian anarchists
Sacco and Vanzetti . . .

Brown Brothers

IN 1921 Dedham, Mass.—some 40 miles from Salem of the infamous seventeenth-century witchcraft trials—was the scene of what many people came to call the "new witch trials". The victims this time were two poor but radical Italian immigrants, Nicola Sacco and Bartolomeo Vanzetti, a shoemaker and fishpeddler.

It is an ironic and sad fact that Sacco and Vanzetti, anarchist idealists, should have fallen, indirectly, victims to the Russian Revolution of 1917. One of the most appalling reverberations of that revolution was the "red scare" it inspired in "capitalist" nations. And no nation seemed more affected by this particularly virulent and vicious social disease than the United States. For the other side of the Jazz Age of the 20's was the cruel mob hysteria that saw evil sorcery in the slightest shade of red.

Sacco and Vanzetti were known radicals who already had an impressive record of strike leadership behind them. They were also foreign and spoke English badly with pronounced Italian accents. It almost seemed natural then for Chief of Police Michael Stewart, who saw all evil as the work of "commies", to arrest Sacco and Vanzetti for a particularly brutal payroll robbery and double murder that had taken place in South Braintree, Mass., on April 15, 1920. In September Sacco and Vanzetti were indicted by a grand jury.

From the start the chief prosecuting attorney, Frederick Katzmann, was determined to crucify "those damned God-hating radicals". He had in this objective the support of 12 conservative jurors and a judge, Webster Thayer, who boasted after the trial, "Did you see what I did with those anarchist bastards the other day?"

But the defendants' troubles did not stop with a hostile judge and jury. In desperation at the calamity that had befallen them they turned towards an anarchist group in New York for help. They were advised to take on Fred Moore as leading counsel for the defence. No choice could have been more ill-advised. Fred Moore may have been a capable lawyer, but he was anathema to the jurors he was trying to convince of Sacco and Vanzetti's innocence.

First of all he was an outsider, brought in from California. Jurors in rural areas tend to resent preference given to outside lawyers over their own bar. But worse than that he came to the trial with a

DID THEY KILL? Vanzetti (left) and Sacco and the guns they had when police arrested them. The photograph of the cartridge case shows breech markings (and firing-pin indentations) which were compared with a test cartridge from Sacco's automatic.

THE BOASTER . . . Judge Webster Thayer. "Did you see what I did with those anarchist bastards the other day?" he asked friends.

reputation as a dyed-in-the-wool radical. He flaunted his bohemian ways in the face of judge and jury. He wore his hair long, dressed outlandishly, and at times was even seen to be lounging outside the courtroom in bare feet.

Further, his headquarters became the rendezvous of assorted offbeat people. Rumours quickly spread of sexual excesses, and the people of Dedham, near the backwoods of New England, were prepared to believe anything of the godless and unscrupulous radical. Subsequent attempts to remove Moore from the case proved fruitless, and it was a tearful Mrs. Sacco who attended the first day proceedings. She had just been told that the defendants were stuck with Moore.

Political arena

Moore's courtroom tactics were to turn the trial into a political arena. From the start he was set on a course of confrontation. And even though at the last moment he had retained the services of the eminently respectable McAnarney brothers, he retained complete control over the direction of the trial.

On vital points he refused to listen to the advice of his fellow attorneys, preferring to follow his political inclinations. Thus, in selecting a jury he went through nearly 700 prospective jurors, refusing automatically anyone who worked in a bank or brokerage house. Thomas McAnarney said a few years later that "every time I wanted a man on the jury whom I felt to be honest he would make an exception to it. Whenever he was addressing the court it was quite similar to waving a red flag in the face of a bull".

The effect on Judge Thayer was im-

mediate and disastrous. As John McAnarney told it to the Massachusetts Governor's Advisory Committee set up to review the case in 1927: "This man Moore got under his (Thayer's) skin . . . to such an extent and so irritated him, so that people around could see his reaction on the jury." More than once in the course of the trial Thayer would overrule an objection by Moore with the comment, "Your goose is cooked."

After the first day of the trial John McAnarney, very agitated by the day's proceedings called on a fellow member of the bar, William G. Thompson. It was late at night and Thompson had been sleeping. But McAnarney had to see him for he wanted Thompson to take charge of the defence of Sacco and Vanzetti. Into the early hours of the morning he pleaded with Thompson "to come out on the case. I told him that the lives of two innocent men were at stake." Finally Thompson yielded, but to no avail. Moore categorically refused to withdraw.

After a week of empanelling the jury Fred Katzmann opened the case for the prosecution. He began by reviewing the events of the crime. Cashier Frederick A. Parmenter and his guard Alexander Berardelli were performing their weekly task of transferring the payroll of the Slater and Morrill Shoe Company—amounting to nearly $16,000—from one factory to another along the main street of South Braintree.

It was about three o'clock on that fine spring afternoon. There was nothing sinister to be seen or sensed. People dotted the main street; there were a few shoppers; some workers out on business; and two men leaning against the fence of the Rice and Hutchins Company between the two Morrill factories.

Berardelli moved closer to the curb in order to pass the two men. Suddenly a gun was sticking in his ribs, shots were fired, and he crumpled into the gutter. Parmenter, who had been trailing behind Berardelli, dropped his money bag and began to run across the street. The gunman gave chase and brought him down with two shots. Meanwhile, the second bandit had approached Berardelli, put some more bullets into him, and had then fired into the air. A car came careering around the corner. The robbers threw the money bags into the vehicle and pushed themselves in after it. The car quickly sped off. The whole affair lasted a matter of minutes.

Four months earlier on the morning of Christmas Eve 1919, there had been an attempted holdup in the streets of Bridgewater, a manufacturing town some 30 miles south of Boston. A truck carrying the wages of the employees of the White Shoe Company was held up by a car in which sat a party of foreign looking men,

UPI

THE ALIBI . . . Sacco claimed he was taking the family picture (left) to the Italian consul at the time of the killing. Demonstrators (right) protested at the death sentence and Vanzetti's sister broadcast a mercy plea.

whom several witnesses swore to be Italian. Two of these men fired, one with a shotgun, at the driver of the truck—who, being armed, returned their fire. The bandits then concluded that their attempt must fail, and they accordingly drove off. In the course of their inquiries the Bridgewater police found an Overland car in a local garage which had been brought in for repairs. The police believed that it was owned, or was being driven, by an Italian named Boda for the purposes of the attempted holdup. They told Mr. and Mrs. Johnson, who ran the garage, to let them know immediately anyone came in for the automobile.

Two days after the South Braintree holdup a Buick car was found abandoned in a wood not far away. Leading from it were the tracks of a smaller vehicle—which the police felt might be those of the Overland which had been left in the Johnsons' garage. As for the Buick, this was known to have been stolen in the previous November, while its number plates were also taken. The police were convinced that it had been used both at Bridgewater and South Braintree.

On the evening of May 5, Boda called at the garage to collect his car. He was allegedly accompanied by Sacco and Vanzetti and a third Italian named Orciani. While Boda was talking to Mr. Johnson, Mrs. Johnson—under the pretext of fetching some milk—went into the house of a neighbour and telephoned the police. Her husband pointed out to Boda that the car did not have proper licence plates, and either because of this or because (as was alleged by the prosecution) the men realized that Mrs. Johnson was telephoning the police, the Italians left without the Overland—Boda and Orciani on a motorcycle and the other two on foot.

Later that evening Sacco and Vanzetti were arrested on a streetcar and both were found to be armed with revolvers.

The following specimen of compromising literature· was also found in Sacco's possession at the time of his arrest and was later produced at his trial:

Fellow workers, you have fought all the wars. You have worked for all the capitalists. You have wandered over all the countries. Have you harvested the fruits of your labors, the price of your victories? Does the past comfort you? Does the present smile on you? Does the future promise you anything? Have you found a piece of land where you can live like a human being?

On these questions, on this argument, and on this theme the struggle for existence Bartolomeo Vanzetti will speak. Admission free. Freedom of discussion to all. Take the ladies with you.

They were escorted to the local police station, where they were charged with being in possession of firearms without a permit, to which they pleaded guilty. They were also asked their reason for visiting Bridgewater that evening, and about their whereabouts on various other dates. Nothing was said of the two outrages for the time being, although the newspapers began to speculate about their possible participation in them. Boda and Orciano were also picked up, but were allowed to go after questioning—Boda departing hurriedly for Italy, and Orciano satisfying the police that he had been at work on the days of both crimes.

Took a day off

While Sacco and Vanzetti were being held in custody, witnesses who had been at Bridgewater and South Braintree were brought in to identify them. Sacco was able to prove that he had been working in his factory on the previous Christmas Eve, so that he could not be charged with the Bridgewater crime. Unfortunately for him, however, he had had the day off on April 15, and so he was charged with the South Braintree murders. Vanzetti, being a self-employed fishpeddler at Plymouth, was unable to produce an alibi for either day and so he was charged with both crimes. Since the two crimes had been committed in different counties of Massachusetts—Plymouth and Norfolk—the respective indictments were presented by different grand juries.

It was afterwards suggested by the defence that the prosecution deliberately arranged for the Bridgewater case against

Vanzetti to be tried first in the hope that he might be convicted, and when he came up for the second trial with his codefendant, Sacco, the latter might be regarded as under a cloud.

However, the prosecution pointed out that the Plymouth grand jury happened to be in session and could indict Vanzetti at once, whereas the Norfolk grand jury was not due to meet before September. As it turned out Vanzetti was indicted without delay, and stood trial for the attempted holdup in Bridgewater before Judge Webster Thayer at Plymouth on June 22, 1920. On the flimsiest of evidence, he was convicted and sentenced to 10-15 years' imprisonment.

After the history of the affair had been gone over, Katzmann proceeded to call witnesses who identified Sacco and Vanzetti as the robbers in question. There were numerous eyewitnesses to the shooting, none of whom when questioned immediately after the crime could give clear descriptions of the bandits. At the trial, under the subtle prodding of the prosecuting attorney, these witnesses were convinced that the men they saw in the flash of events 13 months previously were the same as those sitting in the dock.

Typical was the testimony of Michael Levangie, gate tender at the South Braintree railroad crossing at the time the murder car had made its escape. In an interview with a reporter for the *Boston Globe* just after the shooting Levangie stated: "I saw nobody, I was too damn scared to see anyone. All I saw was the muzzle of that damn gun and I turned and ran for the shanty and they put a bullet through the shanty."

A different story

In the courtroom, however, Levangie gave a rather different story. Led by the Assistant Prosecuting Attorney Harold P. Williams he let it be known that he had seen one man in the getaway car. The man was driving the car, and he was "dark complected, with cheekbones sticking out, black hair, heavy brown moustache, slouch hat, and army coat".

"Have you seen that man since," asked Williams. "Yes, sir," replied the eager-to-please witness. "Right there!" He pointed to Vanzetti, whose moustache was his trademark. "The one with the moustache. Right in the cage."

It didn't take long for the defence to demolish Levangie's testimony. Too many other witnesses had identified the driver of the car as being sallow and blond. Remarkably, however, Katzmann insisted on pushing Levangie's testimony. In his summation speech to the jury he put the following rhetorical question: "Is his (Levangie's) testimony to be rejected if it disagrees with everybody else if you are satisfied he honestly meant to tell the truth?" Even false testimony would be pressed into service for the task of obtaining a conviction.

There were other witnesses that would not be bullied into a doubtful identification. One such was shoemaker Lewis L. Wade. He was put on the stand as a prosecution witness to identify Sacco. It was an astonished prosecutor who heard this witness say, "Well, I ain't so sure now. I have a little doubt."

Wade's personal courage in refusing to testify falsely had an unhappy ending. A few weeks after he had taken the stand he was dismissed by Slater and Morrill where he had been an employee for 16 years. Wade never doubted as to why.

Conflicting evidence

The trial next exhibited a mass of conflicting testimony on the identity question—59 witnesses going on the witness stand for the prosecution, and 99 for the defence. Mrs. Johnson, for example, was positive that Sacco was one of the men who called at the garage on the evening of his arrest. Another important prosecution witness was the policeman who arrested the prisoners on the street car. He described how he boarded the car and asked them where they came from.

"I said, 'What was you doing in Bridgewater?' They said, 'We went down to see a friend of mine.' I said, 'Who is your friend?' He said, 'A man by the name of Poppy.' 'Well,' I said, 'I want you, you are under arrest.'" Then, according to the police witness, Vanzetti put his hand in his hip pocket, and the policeman said, "Keep your hands out on your lap or you will be sorry." At this point, Vanzetti in the dock shouted at the witness, "You are a liar!" As to Sacco, according to this witness, he denied having a gun on him when he and his companion were arrested as "suspicious characters"—although, in fact, they were both armed.

The local police chief testified that Sacco and Vanzetti denied knowing Boda, the owner of the Overland car, or visiting the Johnson garage. He went on to recall his conversation with Sacco at the time about his automatic.

"You had an automatic in your pocket when arrested?"

"Yes," answered Sacco.

"Why did you carry it?"

"To protect myself. Lots of bad men."

"Why did you carry so many cartridges?"

"Well, I go to see my friend. We go into the woods and fire them."

A cap picked up at the scene of the murder was produced by the prosecution and stated to belong to Sacco, who denied owning it. Two firearms experts were also called. One of them stated that in his

opinion the fatal bullet in each instance had been fired by Sacco's revolver; the other stated that the bullet was "consistent" with having been fired by his revolver. Sacco's employer testified to his good reputation as a steady worker. But he had to admit that Sacco had not been at work on the day of the murders.

For the defence other firearms experts

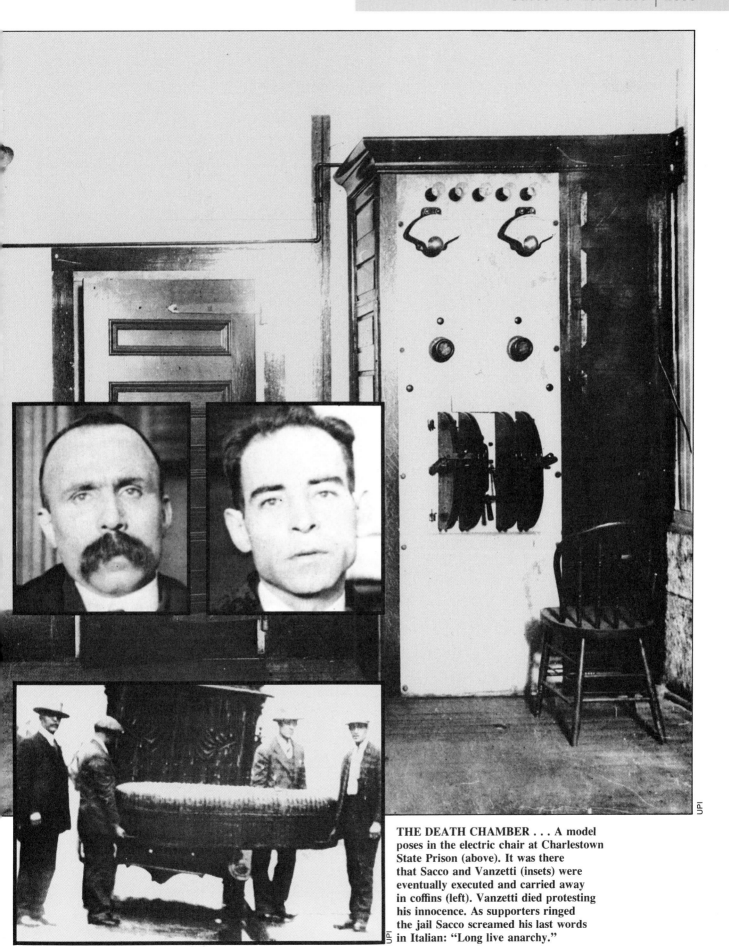

UPI

UPI

THE DEATH CHAMBER . . . A model poses in the electric chair at Charlestown State Prison (above). It was there that Sacco and Vanzetti (insets) were eventually executed and carried away in coffins (left). Vanzetti died protesting his innocence. As supporters ringed the jail Sacco screamed his last words in Italian: "Long live anarchy."

testified that in their view the bullets had not been fired by Sacco's revolver. Otherwise the evidence called by the defence was designed to prove an alibi for both prisoners. In Sacco's case, he swore he had gone to the Italian consulate in Boston on the day of the murders to arrange for a passport to return to Italy. A deposition in support of this was taken in Italy from a clerk who had formerly worked in the consul's office.

Anarchist literature

Other witnesses, mostly Italian, were called to state that, although they had seen the murderers, they were not Sacco and Vanzetti.

Both prisoners testified in their own defence. Vanzetti, who took the stand first, admitted that he had been to the Johnsons' garage on the night of his arrest, although he had previously denied this. Asked why he wanted to use Boda's car, he replied that it was to move a supply of anarchist literature to a safer place than his home and the homes of friends. This was the first mention in the case of his and his codefendant's political opinions, and was deliberately introduced by the defence in order to provide the most convincing answer to the prosecution's case.

Vanzetti went on to explain why he had lied to the police when he was arrested. "Because in that time there was a deportation," he said, "and the reaction was more vivid than now and more mad than now." Both he and Sacco had lied, he stated, because they would be liable to be deported if it were known that they had fled to Mexico in 1917 in order to evade military service. As for lying about the revolver, Vanzetti said he had not wanted to incriminate his friends—from one of whom he had bought it four years previously in Boston.

"It was a very bad time," he said; he had armed himself in self-defence especially because he had to take money, a hundred dollars at a time, to Boston to buy fish.

Sacco's reason for lying to the police was similar to Vanzetti's. "I know some—most of the friends—Socialists, why they are slackers." Sacco used the term "slacker" to connote the English term "conscientious objector" in wartime. "They got literature in the house. They got papers and everything—Socialist movement. That is why I thought they would do the same way as in New York and Chicago."

On the 37th day of the trial, Judge Thayer summed up the evidence quite fairly and dispassionately, and it is diffi-

cult to fault his directions to the jury—although he was subsequently the target for much abuse.

On July 14, 1921, the jury found both Sacco and Vanzetti guilty of murder in the first degree. *"Siamo innocenti,"* cried Sacco from the dock, raising his hand. "They kill an innocent man. They kill two innocent men." They were not brought up to hear Judge Thayer pronounce the death sentence until November 1—a lengthy adjournment necessitated by the appeal procedure.

It was the first of a series of delays, which culminated in the death house of Charlestown Prison seven years later. The inordinately long delay in the Sacco-Vanzetti trial was due to the efforts of their supporters—including their legal advisers—in exhausting every device to save their lives by way of motions for new trials and stays of execution. In deference to public agitation Governor Fuller of Massachusetts appointed an independent committee presided over by President Lowell of Harvard University. But the Lowell Committee found after prolonged investigation that Sacco and Vanzetti were guilty of the South Braintree murders "beyond all reasonable doubt."

Meanwhile a young Portuguese gunman, Celestino Madeiros, confessed to being implicated in the crime and declared that Sacco and Vanzetti were not. However, the Supreme Court of Massachusetts confirmed Judge Thayer's finding that Madeiros's confession fell short of establishing his guilt, or in creating reasonable doubt about the guilt of Sacco and Vanzetti. This judgment was handed down on April 5, 1927, and two days later the prisoners were brought up again to hear the death sentence confirmed.

"You know I am innocent," declared Sacco from the dock. "That is the same words I pronounced seven years ago. You condemn two innocent men." When it came to Vanzetti's turn to speak, he said: "Never in our full life could we hope to do such work for tolerance, for justice, for man's understanding of man as we now do by accident. Our words—our lives—our pains—nothing! The taking of our lives—lives of a good shoemaker and a poor fishpeddler—all! That last moment belongs to us—that agony is our triumph!"

Still the defence persisted in its efforts. After two Federal judges had refused to issue a writ of *Habeas Corpus*, Sacco and Vanzetti were made ready for electrocution on the evening of August 10, 1927. Their trousers had already been slit and their hair cut to facilitate the passage of the electric current through their bodies, when news came that Governor Fuller had postponed the execution for 12 days.

House of death

Also in the death house at this time was Madeiros, who had been sentenced for another murder. Shortly after midnight on August 23, Madeiros, Sacco, and Vanzetti were executed in that order, while the jail was surrounded by machine guns and besieged by a crowd of excited sightseers and partisans.

Sacco's last words were, "Long live anarchy!" in Italian, and in English: "Farewell my wife and child and all my friends. Farewell, mother." Vanzetti protested his innocence to the last: "I have never committed any crime but sometimes some sin . . . I am innocent of all crime, not only of this, but all."

It was the Italians' long wait for death that shocked and revolted millions of people throughout the world. The entire case was a blot on the record book of American legal procedure and justice.

THE LAST TRIBUTE . . . Thousands of supporters line the route as Sacco and Vanzetti are buried. Their long wait for death shocked the world.

UPI

'NOT FROM VAINGLORY . . .'

In the rough-and-tumble Tuapeka goldfields it was every man for himself.

THE three men in the prisoners' dock stared malevolently at the man in the witness-box, who had solemnly sworn to tell the truth, the whole truth and nothing but the truth. Their bodies twitched as if they wanted to spring across the court-room and tear the life from the witness who, in their criminal code, had committed the worst crime of all—far worse than the terrible crimes with which they themselves stood charged.

For this man had shared a part, with the three prisoners, in murder—and he now sought to save himself by turning betrayer.

The Supreme Court, in the small New Zealand seaport town of Nelson, was crowded that September day in 1866. People had been drawn there by shock and anger at events three months earlier, when five gold prospectors had been ambushed on a deserted path on Maungatapu—the mountain sacred to the Maoris on the South Island of New Zealand—and their dead bodies concealed in bracken and under brushwood.

The Crown contended that the deed had been committed by the three men in the dock: Richard Burgess (real name Hill), Tom Kelly (real name Noon) and Philip Levy. The witness, Joe Sullivan, was, like the others, a dedicated, professional criminal.

They had leapt upon the prospectors as they cautiously drove their heavily-laden pack horses among the rocks and boulders of the mountainside. They then bound their victims, took them one by one a few yards away into the bush, and there killed them by strangling and knifing.

They were not the first men in that part of the country to rob hard-working miners of their gold. But they were the first to murder—to ensure, so they hoped, that there would be no witness left alive to identify them and bring them to justice.

But Joe Sullivan had knocked the props from under that. He had gabbled out the "terrible story" to the authorities, and had thus escaped indictment for his part in the killings. Burgess, alone among the other three, had confessed to his role, and it came as a surprise to many in the courtroom when he entered his plea.

For the sake of form

"I have already acknowledged before God and the public that I am guilty of these awful murders, and I do not mean to depart from that now, but for the sake of form I shall plead not guilty!"

His reason for the curious "not guilty" plea soon became apparent. Burgess was determined to question Sullivan in open court, and so blacken his character as thoroughly as he could. A formal guilty plea would have deprived him of that opportunity.

"Now, Burgess," commanded the judge, His Honour Mr. Justice Alexander Johnston, from Wellington, "it is your time to cross-examine the witness."

The diminutive Richard Burgess—only 5 feet 4½ inches high—turned his gaze upon Sullivan. For the moment, however, the spectators fastened their eyes on Burgess. There was clearly a certain animal cunning in the man. His drooping moustache and profuse mutton-chop side-whiskers made him look particularly sinister. He carried with him the air of rotting ships' hulks in the far-away Thames Estuary, and reminders of white men's slavery in the British Empire's colonies.

For this was only 20 years after the days of transportation, when Britain combed through her festering, over-crowded jails and sent convicts to work as slaves in the penal settlements of Australia's New South Wales.

Burgess had been transported, in May 1847, under a new and cynical system devised by the British authorities. By then men were no longer being sent to Australia officially as prisoners. If they had been classified in the jails as "good conduct" men they were exiled to New South Wales. There they were given a conditional pardon and released. The condition was that they could not return to England until the term of their sentences had expired.

It was a useful way of recruiting labour for the colony's growing sheep-farming industry; and since the authorities had no intention of paying return fares, few, if any, men ever saw their homeland again.

Burgess had been convicted of robbery back in Britain. Although he had had the chance of making an honest living in Australia, and even of prospering, he had continued with his "life of crime". Finally, he took himself and his campaign against law-abiding society across to New Zealand—where it now seemed that he was but a few steps from the gallows.

A touch of asperity

"What I wish to do is merely to forward the ends of justice," he said quietly. The judge replied with a touch of asperity. "The court cannot admit that you are here as an advocate of justice. You are a prisoner on trial for a capital offence. You have admitted being guilty, yet pleaded not guilty, in order to have an opportunity of accusing another."

There was a quickening of interest as the crowd in the courtroom sought the meaning behind the judge's words. But complete silence fell as the 37-year-old Burgess began, with apparent nonchalance, to question Sullivan. He established that Sullivan had arrived in the colonies

SHOCK AND ANGER drew crowds of spectators to the sleepy seaport town on the South Island. One of the first murder trials in New Zealand was held in Nelson.

Illustrated London News

The Graphic

in 1840 as a prisoner, that he had been sent to Van Diemen's Land (now Tasmania) for robbery, had escaped and been recaptured. If there had been any doubt in anyone's mind that Joe Sullivan was a hardened criminal, it was dispelled in Burgess's first few minutes of questions.

"Why," Burgess demanded, "did you murder that poor unfortunate man, Mr. Battle?" Sullivan licked his lips, nervously. Burgess and his gang, including Sullivan, were jointly suspected of murdering old Jamie Battle, a sailor known to carry considerable sums of money around with him.

The killing was not part of the indictment, but it was evident that even if Sullivan might escape punishment for the deaths of the prospectors, Burgess would do his best to see him hanged for Jamie Battle's death. Sullivan spoke up sharply, slightly hysterically. "I did not murder Mr. Battle, nor did I see the murder!"

"Did you tell the police where the body of Battle was to be found?" Burgess demanded. "No!" shouted Sullivan, his bearded chin shaking with agitation. "I stated the locality," he added lamely, subdued by the scornful sniggers of the men in the dock. Burgess paused briefly and then posed the question: "If you had

not been arrested, would you have given information to the police?" "Yes," came the brisk answer. But it was evident to lawyers and jury that the reply carried little conviction.

Burgess had achieved as much as he could hope for, and soon the role of interrogator passed to Tom Kelly. Like Burgess, Kelly was London-born, 39, a one-time tailor's apprentice, sentenced to seven years' transportation in 1842. Again, like Burgess, he sported a thick, drooping moustache and mutton-chop whiskers. He, too, proved to be a man of some intelligence, and with enough experience of courtroom procedure to select and weigh his questions. As Kelly rose from his seat in the dock, Sullivan began to sweat with apprehension.

A touch of bravado

"What did you make your confession, and give your information for?" Kelly demanded. Sullivan tried a touch of bravado. "To endeavour to bring you to justice, and convict you if possible!" But why, after his arrest, had he waited for eight days before informing to the authorities? Sullivan looked around uneasily, began to reply, swallowed his words and subsided into silence. Kelly

A MINER'S LOT: "Exposed to the hail and the rain, the forest and the sunshine, the fowls of the air and the beasts of the field, the wild pigs and the rats . . ."

roared at him:

"Why did you leave five of your fellow-creatures on the top of a high mountain, exposed to the hail and the rain, the frost and the sunshine, and exposed to the fowls of the air and the beasts of the field —the wild pigs and the rats, with which many parts of the jungle of New Zealand are infested, and thus allow the bodies to be exposed for so long a time, before you made your confession?"

"Because it was not safe to confess at once," Sullivan whined, "and as for the bodies, the mischief had been done and they were dead!" Kelly sneered at his former companion-in-crime. "Is it not a fact that you will swear to anything you like? "No," Sullivan protested, looking to the judge for support. "I shall swear to the truth and nothing else."

Next, one of the defence counsel reminded Sullivan of the wording of a notice posted when the prospectors were still reported as missing, and before the discovery of their bodies:

"This is to notify that should those

persons, or any of them, have been murdered, A REWARD OF TWO HUNDRED POUNDS will be given to any person who will give information that will lead to the conviction of the perpetrators: or His Excellency the Governor will grant A FREE PARDON to any person implicated in such murder, except to the actual murderer or murderers, who shall give such information as shall lead to the conviction aforesaid."

Sullivan was indignant at the implication. He had certainly not turned informer for money, he declared; indeed, he had not even seen the reward notice before he went to the authorities.

The most dramatic aspect of the trial, for which everyone was eagerly waiting, was Richard Burgess's own remarkable confession. It had been given widespread publicity in the pre-trial proceedings, but now the moment came when Burgess was to present it as evidence and address the jury upon it. But, first, the judge entered a note of caution. He told Burgess:

"It is a most extraordinary proceeding that a man should plead not guilty and then tell the court and the jury that he is guilty. I must warn you, Burgess, that I shall direct the jury to pay not the slightest attention to anything that you might say, out of a wretched vainglory, that does not concern the evidence that has been given."

Burgess made a brief bow to the judge, then, in even tones, he stated: "My object in disclosing my own blood-guiltiness is so that innocent men should not suffer. I stand here, an actual murderer, and I state this, not from vainglory, but because I wish to clear the innocent men accused of the murders which I and the villain Sullivan committed."

Ultimate sacrifice

There was a buzz of subdued chatter in the courtroom as spectators grasped the emerging pattern of the trial. Here was a man who was admitting to an act that must, beyond doubt, end in his own execution. He was doing so in order to implicate the informer. In short, he was

ready to sacrifice his own life to express his loathing for the sin of betrayal.

Burgess warmed to his task. "I loathe myself when I think of my misdeeds," he declared. "I stand before you as an execrable being, one who has destroyed the image of his Maker, and therefore I wish to make now what reparation I can. Sullivan, in his endeavour to free himself, has accused innocent men. He steps into the witness-box and stands before you as a very fiend.

"I should not have cared for his confession against me, for my own life is forfeited, for I am a principal agent in this terrible tragedy, and so is he. I know that my name shall be remembered hereafter amidst the execrations of my fellowmen, but it is my intention to aid you to see through this mysterious case."

As Burgess gave his account of the murders, only he and Sullivan were involved. The two of them, he insisted, had ambushed the prospectors' party, and, while Burgess kept the men covered with his gun, Sullivan tied their hands behind their backs. Then, when the victims had been taken into the bush, he and Sullivan shared equally in the killings. It was not until the next day that he and Sullivan caught up, along the mountain trail, with the other two prisoners, Kelly and Levy. Burgess and Sullivan reported that they had robbed a man of gold, but made no mention of the murders.

"Gentlemen," said Burgess, addressing the jury, "Sullivan's motive in giving information was to implicate others and to save himself! He is the veritable murderer, along with myself. I do not wish to incriminate anyone falsely, or to cause anyone to suffer the death penalty. God forbid! I know that I must suffer that penalty. I know that I shall shortly make my exit from this world, and I wish to save the lives of innocent men.

"I have disburdened myself. I have nothing further to disclose. I have cleared myself of the responsibility of doing my best to save the innocent. God who is above knows all. Now, gentlemen, I leave the case to your superior judgment!"

After Burgess, it was Tom Kelly's turn to attack Sullivan. He did so in ringing purple prose, and all eyes turned on the informer. Sullivan looked around him as though grasping for a lifeline. He was thrown one by the judge, who ordered, "Let Sullivan be removed from the court."

After Levy's defence counsel had presented a blanket denial of the murder charge, the trial entered its final day. The courtroom was capacity-packed, and

THE AMBUSH took place on a deserted pathway on Maungatapu — a mountain sacred to the Maoris. The unsuspecting miners were strangled and knifed, and concealed in bracken and brushwood.

SULLIVAN THE INFORMER was set free on condition that he leave New Zealand (and Australia).

promptly at nine o'clock the judge began his last address to the jury. He spoke, with only a short lunchtime break, for six and a half hours.

Burgess he dealt with in only a few words. After all, despite his technical plea of not guilty, he had confessed to the murders, and his statement to the jury, the judge declared, exhibited a "braggart vanity that I have never encountered".

In the cases of Kelly and Levy, His Honour counselled the jury that, even if they had not struck one blow but had conspired in robbery-with-murder, they were accessories before the fact. If they knew what was going on and were near enough to have aided in the crime in some way, they were guilty as principals in the second degree. One important point, that told against them, was that they had shared in the proceeds of the robbery of the dead prospectors.

As to Sullivan, the judge had this to say: "A great deal of obloquy, and I will say deserved obloquy, has been thrown on the evidence of Sullivan. The jury must consider the circumstances. Here is a man who has taken an active part in the proceedings of the other prisoners. He has made no attempt to extenuate his crime. He has acknowledged his complicity in these deeds. He has now tendered his evidence in order to convict his fellow-criminals.

"There is no doubt that Sullivan was actuated by a hope of the pardon offered by the government to an accomplice who was ready to turn approver, and was not the actual murderer. I cannot see, gentlemen, how it could ever be judicially proved that Sullivan was not one of the actual murderers. . . ."

It took the jury only 55 minutes to consider their verdicts and find all three prisoners guilty. The judge donned the black cap, and he had barely pronounced the death sentences when an excited Tom Kelly shouted from the dock: "I was not on the road, nor near to the men when

they were murdered! Your Honour did not charge the jury right when you said that evidence corroborated Sullivan's evidence."

Soon, at a sign from the judge, a policeman took Kelly by the shoulders, forced him to the floor of the dock, and then sat upon him. When Kelly's sobs had subsided, the so-far silent Philip Levy spoke up. "I am happy to inform you," he told the judge in clipped tones, "that in my own mind, and from the very bottom of my heart, by the God I worship, I leave this bar an innocent man!"

Joe Sullivan, the informer, was not a witness to the final, incredible scenes in court. For although he had not been charged with the murders of the prospectors, he still had to stand trial for his part in the killing of the old sailor, Jamie Battle. And that trial opened on the very day after Burgess, Kelly and Levy had been sentenced to death.

He conducted his own defence, and where, in the previous trial, Burgess had accused him of perjury, he now turned the tables and declared that Burgess had lied in accusing Sullivan of Battle's murder. He pleaded that Burgess "exercised a terror-like influence over me".

Duly sentenced

But the new jury dismissed his story, and after only 25 minutes of discussion found him guilty, and he duly was sentenced to death. On Friday, October 5, 1866, Burgess, Kelly, and Levy were hanged in the jail yard at Nelson by a masked hangman, especially shipped in from Wellington for the occasion. Kelly and Levy wept and begged that their lives might be spared. Burgess mounted the scaffold calmly and told the sheriff: "I am ready to obey the commands of the law. I pray that God will have mercy on my soul."

Observers at the execution had the impression that Burgess was going contentedly to his death, confident in the knowledge that his betrayer would soon be joining him. Had he known the truth he, too, might have cried out against the hangman. For his hated, former associate, Sullivan, survived.

The embarrassed authorities, having pardoned Sullivan for his part in the prospectors' murders, felt that it might seem like sharp practice if they still insisted on taking his life for the killing of Jamie Battle. His sentence was commuted to one of life imprisonment. In 1874 he was set free on condition that he left New Zealand and never went to Australia.

Sullivan went to England, was harried there by the police and made his way, despite his conditional release, to Melbourne, Australia. There he was picked up by the police and arrested as a person "being illegally at large" in the colony.

POLICE ORGANIZATION

'If a man has knocked out the teeth of a man of the same rank, his own teeth shall be knocked out.' This unbending rule was part of the Code of law published by Hammurabi, the king of Babylon, some 2000 years BC. The code was strong on crime and punishment but relied on citizens being prepared to tell the truth on oath. In cases of doubt, trial by ordeal usually settled a person's guilt. The idea of voluntary obedience to the law was widely shared in both ancient and modern worlds and enforcement was a matter for each community.

Above: *In this method of trial by ordeal, the accused was innocent if he sank, and guilty if he floated.*

In England after the Norman Conquest, every man was held responsible for his behaviour and it was his duty to take action on any crime he saw committed. A 'hue and cry' was raised and he called on his neighbours to assist in pursuit of the miscreant. In time, families were grouped ten to a tithing and ten tithings became a hundred which was presided over by a constable, usually a nobleman, who had charge of the hundred's weapons.

Eventually, hundreds were formed into shires, areas with geographical boundaries, and the Crown appointed a shire reeve (Sheriff) to look after its interests which included law and order. The principal judicial and political institutions grew out of this system, including Common Law, which was based on custom and precedent and was the same for all members of society, trial by jury and habeas corpus which safeguarded the individual from unlawful detention.

Upholding of the law by the people because they believed in it worked effectively when society consisted of small communities in which infractions of discipline were easily observed. The steady growth of industrialization and development of large cities created a different social structure in which the old methods of regulating behaviour broke down. Faster communications and transportation aided this process and crime became more anonymous with pick-pockets and thieves of all kinds infesting the towns and highway robbers molesting travellers. The need for organized enforcement of the law had dawned.

The English police

Police organization in England dates from 1829 when Sir Robert Peel (1788-1850), the Home Secretary, established the Metropolitan Police Force. Much of the groundwork had been laid by Henry Fielding (1707-1754), the novelist, who became an unpaid police magistrate at Bow Street in 1748 at a time when London's streets were unsafe for the ordinary citizen. Bands of robbers were at large, usually at night, and their antics proved too much for the handful of parish constables who opposed them. Practically the only antidotes to crime at that time were the 'hue and cry' and the thief-takers who responded to a reward system.

Above: *A Bow Street Runner of 1804. They served as detectives until 1829, being replaced by 'Peelers'.*
Below: *Jonathan Wild on his way to Tyburn. He was a thief and receiver of stolen goods in London, and betrayed other thieves who would not share with him.*

The Bow Street Runners

Fielding decided to improve this situation by organizing a small group of six willing men who operated as plain-clothes detectives. These were the famous Bow Street Runners who had neither official status nor remuneration but who quickly won acclaim by ridding the streets of thieves. So successful were they that Fielding persuaded the government to pay each man a guinea a week from the Secret Service Fund to supplement his earnings as a thief-taker.

The Highwayman Act of 1692 provided a reward of £40 for the arrest and prosecution of any highwayman and a scale of fees for apprehending house-breakers, counterfeiters, army deserters and other miscreants. The most successful member of the profession of thief-takers was Jonathan Wild who sent over a hundred men to the gallows before he too trod the scaffold in 1725. Many thief-takers were themselves criminals and their inspiration had less to do with public service than with personal gain.

It was against this background that Henry Fielding organized his Bow Street Runners and in 1792 opened seven other offices in London each staffed with Runners. Some recognition came in 1800 when two Bow Street Runners were detailed as royal protectors following the assassination attempt on George II by James Hadfield at Drury Lane Theatre. Elsewhere in England at that time, law enforcement was carried out by constables and watchmen appointed by individual parishes. Fielding's maxim was 'quick notice and sudden pursuit', the chase being the forte of his Runners. He advertised in the newspapers urging the public to report criminal acts with speed while the trail was still warm. He showed considerable vision in setting up criminal records and advocating exchanges of information between police magistrates throughout the country.

Henry Fielding died before he could put all his ideas into practice and he was succeeded by his half brother, John, who had been blind since youth. John Fielding was a magistrate for over a quarter of a century and despite his handicap carried on his predecessor's work with great distinction. Sir John, as he later became, was also a pioneer in his own right, starting foot patrols and founding the journal *Hue and Cry* which later became the *Police Gazette*.

Between them, Henry and John Fielding established high standards for the conduct of magistrates and exhibited vision and humanity in equal proportions.

Twelve years after Sir John's death, Patrick Colquhoun (1745-1820), Lord Provost of Glasgow, retired to London where he was appointed a magistrate. He published *A Treatise on the Police of the Metropolis* which was a blueprint for police organization. He suggested that a police force be set up under the Home Office and advocated establishing a criminal record office and an official police journal.

Robert Peel's act
Thus, when the Home Secretary, Sir Robert Peel, put before Parliament in 1829 a bill 'for improving the police in and near the Metropolis', he was standing on ground that had been well prepared. Despite keen opposition, the bill became law and England's

Above: *Peel reformed the archaic penal code and simultaneously created a regular police force, the 'Peelers'* (below), *who wore beards to enhance their authority.*

Above: *Fielding, the second Bow Street magistrate after Sir Thomas de Veil was the equivalent of the present-day Metropolitan Police Commissioner.*

first official police force was created. A thousand uniformed men, nick-named 'Blue Devils' or 'Bobbies', went on patrol in London's streets. Peel had sought to ensure the impartiality of the police through their immunity from politics and by making them subject to the laws which they enforced. This independent character of the British police system is a feature which has distinguished it from the systems used in other countries.

The Metropolitan Police Force

The newly formed Metropolitan Police Force was headed by two justices of the peace or Commissioners who built up the force's strength to 3000 men. Sir Richard Mayne and Sir Charles Rowan, combining the respective disciplines of lawyer and army officer, established in practice that the police were truly servants of the public. Sir Richard said that 'the protection of life and property, the preservation of public tranquillity and the absence of

crime' would decide whether the police attained their objectives.

The extent to which the Metropolitan Police succeeded may be judged from the fact that in 1856 Parliament passed legislation making the provision of police forces throughout England and Wales compulsory. Scotland had its own legislation in the following year.

From its inception, the Metropolitan Police set up its headquarters office in Westminster in buildings entered through Great Scotland Yard. This centre of police activity in London was soon called 'Scotland Yard', a name which was to become known throughout the world as a symbol of the English policing system. The name remained even when the headquarters location was changed – it simply became New Scotland Yard.

Organizing the British police

At the same time that a police system was established throughout Britain, the Metropolitan Police Force was put under the command of a single Commissioner. He is appointed by the Crown on the advice of the Home Secretary. The Metropolitan force is the largest in the country with about a quarter of the total police manpower in the country. Its district is very large, and includes two whole counties and parts of four others.

In addition to policing the greater London area, the Metropolitan force has a number of national responsibilities. These are the maintenance of criminal records including fingerprints for the whole country, running the national bureau for Interpol, VIP protection and provision of criminal investigation expertise when required by other police forces.

The Commissioner of Police of the Metropolis has a Deputy Commissioner and four Assistant Commissioners (ACs) working under him. Each AC is responsible for a particular branch of police activity such as traffic, criminal investigation, administration and training. The Metropolitan Police area is divided into a number of districts, containing 23 divisions each under a Chief Superintendent. Up to 1829 the Bow Street Runners continued to carry out detective duties but they were disbanded in that year when the Metropolitan Police formed a small detective branch. This

Right: *The growth of terrorism and bombing, such as this City of London blast by the IRA in 1993, has added another dimension to police work.*

became, in 1878, the Criminal Investigation Department (CID) and it is for this activity that Scotland Yard has become world famous. Over the years it has been traditional for other British police forces to 'call in the Yard' to help solve difficult cases, especially murder investigations. The Criminal Investigation Department runs a number of specialized activities including the Fingerprint and Photographic Branch, Criminal Records, Serious Fraud Office, Drug Squad and Special Branch.

Following the Police Act of 1964, the police system in England and Wales was reorganized. The great number of separate forces was reduced to 47, and later to 43, large units each under the direction of a Chief Constable. These stream-lined forces carry out law enforcement in their areas and, unlike the Metropolitan Police which answers to the Home Secretary, are subject to a local police authority. Each police force has its own CID capability and reorganization provided for improvements in training, equipment and communications, in recognition of the need to deal with developments such as inner city violence and international terrorism.

Technology and communication systems

Police organization in Britain has five major facets consisting of crime prevention; criminal investigation; traffic control; dealing with vice, gambling and narcotics; and juvenile crime. These branches of police work are aided by the use of modern communications and information systems supported by forensic science laboratory facilities. Probably the first piece of technical equipment to be introduced was the police whistle in 1884. Motorized patrols followed with motorcycles in 1921 and cars equipped with two-way radio in 1927. Two-way radio contact is used by every officer on patrol today and mobile units include river craft and helicopters. Recent legislation has added riot protection gear, CS gas, water cannon and personnel carriers. Yet the single feature which sets the British police officer apart from his opposite number elsewhere in

the world is that he is not equipped with a firearm. While this remains true in general, the growth of terrorism has necessitated the carrying of guns by officers involved in special protection duties and greater numbers of officers are being trained in the use of firearms.

Information handling is an important component of any modern organization and the use of computerized on-line search facilities greatly speeds up enquiries. The Police National Computer at Hendon, which cost £50 million to set up, puts the police officer at the scene of enquiry in touch with a wealth of information within minutes. This computer is linked with 500 terminals located at police stations throughout the country and can deal with thousands of enquiries an hour. The system houses

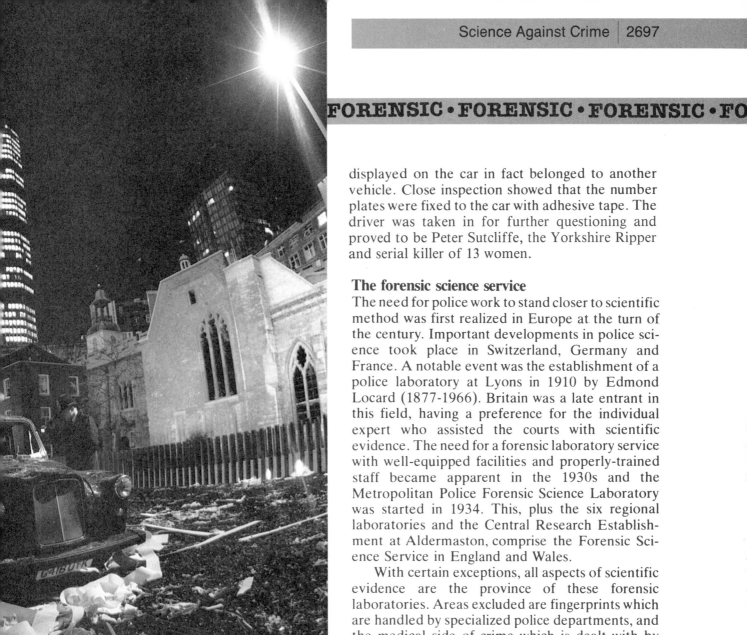

displayed on the car in fact belonged to another vehicle. Close inspection showed that the number plates were fixed to the car with adhesive tape. The driver was taken in for further questioning and proved to be Peter Sutcliffe, the Yorkshire Ripper and serial killer of 13 women.

The forensic science service

The need for police work to stand closer to scientific method was first realized in Europe at the turn of the century. Important developments in police science took place in Switzerland, Germany and France. A notable event was the establishment of a police laboratory at Lyons in 1910 by Edmond Locard (1877-1966). Britain was a late entrant in this field, having a preference for the individual expert who assisted the courts with scientific evidence. The need for a forensic laboratory service with well-equipped facilities and properly-trained staff became apparent in the 1930s and the Metropolitan Police Forensic Science Laboratory was started in 1934. This, plus the six regional laboratories and the Central Research Establishment at Aldermaston, comprise the Forensic Science Service in England and Wales.

With certain exceptions, all aspects of scientific evidence are the province of these forensic laboratories. Areas excluded are fingerprints which are handled by specialized police departments, and the medical side of crime which is dealt with by police surgeons and pathologists retained by the Home Office. Trace materials collected as evidence at scenes of crime represent an enormous array of substances, mostly commonplace, which may yield important information linking a crime and suspect.

These may range from human tissues and body fluids such as skin, hair, blood and semen to such crime debris as broken glass, paint fragments, clothing fibres, bullets, cartridge cases, offensive weapons, explosives, forged documents, drugs and many other crime artifacts. There are also the impressions left by vehicle tyres, footprints and tools in association with every type of crime from arson to violent assault. In the course of a year, the Metropolitan Police Forensic Science Laboratory alone will carry out over 30,000 forensic investigations involving many specialist skills.

information on registered vehicle numbers, disqualified drivers, stolen cars, fingerprints and missing persons.

It was the speed of this information network interacting with the judgement of the man-on-the-spot which led to the capture of the Yorkshire Ripper in January 1981. Two uniformed officers in a patrol car set out on a routine night patrol in Sheffield. Just before 11 pm, they saw a stationary car in what their instincts told them were suspicious circumstances. There were two occupants in the car one of whom was recognized as a prostitute. After questioning the driver, the officers radioed the vehicle's registration number to the local VDU operator for a routine check. The reply justified their suspicion for the registration number

GETTING AWAY WITH MURDER
Brian Donald Hume

The name 'Interpol' evokes romantic associations for many people. They imagine sophisticated Maigret-like sleuths hunting their quarry across international boundaries; gum chewing New York detectives telephoning details of a suspect to London, England, in laconic 'wise guy' accents. There is some foundation for such colourful associations, of course. However, it should be admitted that the real strength of Interpol is based on the thoroughness and efficiency of its classification systems, and on its comprehensive international coverage.

These rather more prosaic qualities were to be the key factors in the downfall of a British criminal who had successfully eluded a murder verdict. Brian Donald Hume was also over-confident of the extent of his legal knowledge, and failed to take the ordinary precaution of checking a simple fact. He firmly and mistakenly believed that Switzerland was not included in the Interpol network because it did not belong to the United Nations.

The story began in January 1950. Hume appeared at London's Old Bailey charged with the murder of Stanley Setty, a shady businessman whose headless torso had been washed up on the Essex mud-flats at Tillingham. It was proved that Hume had flown in a hired light aircraft carrying two parcels around the time Setty disappeared. When questioned, Hume claimed the parcels contained parts of a printing press used to print forged food-ration coupons which he had been asked to dump at sea. Later, he elaborated this story, saying that one of the parcels made a gurgling noise when he moved it and it had crossed his mind that it might be a body – possibly that of Setty who he knew had been reported missing. Due to a technicality, Hume was found not guilty of murder, although he was convicted for being an accessory and received a twelve-year prison sentence.

Having earned all the remission to which he was entitled, Hume left prison in February 1958. In April, he changed his name to Donald Brown and in June sold his story for £2,000 to the *Sunday Pictorial* newspaper which published his confession to the murder of Stanley Setty. He claimed that he attacked Setty with a Nazi SS dagger. He had only intended to frighten him as he believed he was having an affair with his wife. In the course of this assault, it occurred to him, "– perhaps I could get away with murder." He admitted killing Setty, cutting up the body and dumping it in the English Channel from a light aircraft. The *Sunday Pictorial* obviously had a 'scoop' on its hands, and Hume was the centre of a blaze of publicity. Although he knew he could not be tried again for the same crime he decided it would be prudent to lie low for a while. He therefore disguised his appearance and with a pass-

port identifying him as John Steven Bird, chemical engineer, headed for Switzerland with the £2,000 newspaper fee in banknotes.

In Switzerland, he converted his money to US currency and travelled to North America where he enjoyed a spending spree and passed himself off as Johnny Bird, Canadian test-pilot. In July 1958 he returned to Switzerland and in Zurich resumed his relationship with his girl-friend, Trudi Sommer.

Not surprisingly, after his travels, Hume was now short of funds. His remedy was to rob a bank, and where better than England where the authorities would least expect him? He flew to England as Donald Brown, held up a bank in Brentford at gun-point, grabbed £1,300, and returned to Zurich as John Bird.

Eventually, Trudi began pressing him about marriage, and some awkward revelations occurred regarding his passport and various aliases. He decided it was time to travel again and took himself off to Canada. He returned, as before, short of funds and decided on the same solution. Indeed, he planned to rob the same London bank as before but discovered that it had moved. With the dogged determination of the committed criminal, he traced it to its new premises but was rewarded with only poor pickings amounting to £300. He further bungled his escape by leaving his raincoat on a train.

With this garment and aided by descriptions of the bank robber, police were able to connect Donald Brown to the raid and thence to Donald Hume. The only consolation for Hume was that he had seen a Police Wanted Notice which offered £1,000 reward for his capture; "it made me feel good to know I was wanted," he remarked later. He returned to Trudi whose suspicions were aroused when she found he was carrying a gun. She pleaded with him to dispose of it but he had already decided on a further, fatal excursion into armed robbery.

On 30 January 1959, Hume walked into the Gewerbe Bank in Zurich, produced a gun and shot the cashier in the stomach. He grabbed 215 Swiss francs and was prising open a safety drawer when the wounded cashier touched off the alarm which rang in the central police station. Within minutes, police were on the scene and pursuing the robber whom the alarm bells had put to flight. Various passers-by joined in the chase and Arthur Maag, a taxi-driver, dived at his legs. Hume fired and Maag collapsed, fatally injured. Within seconds the fleeing murderer was overwhelmed by a mob of people.

Hume was taken into police custody and questioned but several hours went by before he offered any reply. Then, answering in English, he said he was John Stanilav, a civilian employee at the US Air Force in Wiesbaden. When the police provided a Polish interpreter to allow the arrested man to develop his explanation further, his deception was quickly discovered. The Zurich police sent

SUNDAY PICTORIAL, June 8 1953   PAGE

HUME CONFESSION

'I killed Setty...'

DONALD HUME'S ADMISSION
TO THE PICTORIAL THAT
STARTED WORLD CONTROVERSY

THERE was a blazing row when car dealer Stanley Setty and I met in my flat at Finchley-road, Golders Green, on the evening of October 4, 1949.

It was 7.35 p.m. I was livid with anger at this man for whom I had been earning money by stealing cars.

The cars I stole on his order had to match the log-books of wrecked vehicles he had already bought.

TREMBLE

BUT, furious as I was, I did not know then that seventeen minutes later I would have his dead body—and his blood—on my hands.

I began to tremble with rage when this black marketeer refused to get out.

I saw red. I yelled at him, then ran out on to the landing and snatched a dagger from the collection of war souvenirs on the wall.

DAGGER

THE handle of the dagger glinted in the light. I could see the initials "S.S."

In war, they stood for Schutz Staffel, the elite army corps of Nazi Germany.

Now those S.S. initials stood for forty-four-year-old Stanley Setty.

I dashed, dagger in hand,

I'M HOLDING A DAGGER LIKE THE ONE I USED TO KILL STANLEY SETTY

seemed to come naturally to me. We rolled over and over and my sweaty hand plunged the weapon frenziedly and repeatedly into his chest and legs.

I had to hurt him.

I aimed my blows anywhere. But Setty continued to struggle. He was as strong as an ox.

The more I stuck the dagger into him, the more he tried to push my head back and break my neck.

I tried to push Setty away from me to keep his blood off my clothes and force a gap between us.

I forced my knee into him. He grunted, but he wouldn't release his grip. It was like a vice.

WRITHE

I HELD the knife up to strike the sixth or seventh blow. I can't remember.

I plunged the blade into his ribs. I know I heard them crack.

He sank back against the sofa and slumped on the floor. He writhed and rolled over to a spot to reach the window, on his back.

Setty began to cough violently and a trickle of red came from his mouth as he heaved and panted.

I stood over him with the dagger in my hand.

And, with a feeling of triumph at winning the fight, I watched the life run from him.

I looked at the clock. It was 7.52 p.m. The fight had lasted less than two minutes—about the same time as it took you to read about it.

Now Setty lay on his back, his eyes seemed glassily fixed on the ceiling

knew that Setty had come to my flat?

I fought off my daze. My mind started clicking again.

Down in the streets outside, life was going on as usual. Carefree couples strolled arm in arm on their way to the pictures.

But at my feet a man lay dead . . . murdered by me.

I wandered unsteadily into the back room where Tony, my dog had slept through it all. I wanted time to restore myself to an even balance. I wanted to be able to think straight.

The thought flashed through my mind that perhaps I could get away with murder.

HEAVED

FIRST, I had to get rid of all traces of the killing. Next, I had to get the body out of the way.

I went back into the lounge. Setty still lay on his back, his staring eyes fixed on the ceiling.

I got hold of him by the legs and started to drag him, being careful to keep him on his back so that blood from his chest did not trail on the floor.

He seemed a ton weight. But I dragged him across the hall, right through the dining room and scullery of my flat, and into the breakfast room.

Then I heaved him into the coal cupboard and covered him with an old piece of felt.

TIDIED

NEXT, I tidied up the lounge and set to rights the furni-

off a detailed description of Mr Stanilav to Interpol headquarters in Paris.

Interpol's criminal classification system was put to the test and within an hour it was established that John Stanilav was identical to Donald Brown. The British authorities had notified Interpol in 1958 when Donald Hume changed his name to Brown by deed poll. Thus, the Zurich police now knew that the man they held as Stanilav was in fact Donald Hume, self-confessed murderer of Stanley Setty. Interpol also supplied the information that Hume, in the name of Brown, was wanted in London for two armed bank robberies in August and November 1958.

The extent of Hume's exploits and deception came to light when the Zurich police published his photograph. Trudi Sommer came forward to state that she knew him as John Bird, the man to whom she was engaged to be married. She produced letters which he had sent her from

America and Canada. Hume, alias Brown, alias Bird and sundry other identities was sent to Regendorf prison to await trial for murder.

The trial indictment accused Hume of murder, attempted murder, armed robbery and other crimes to which he pleaded guilty. After due process, the jury convicted him and he was sentenced to life imprisonment with hard labour. Hume said nothing in his own defence but gave a characteristic display of violent struggling when being escorted from the court. Thus, nine years after he killed Setty in London, Hume was brought to book for murder.

He told the Zurich police after he was arrested that he chose Switzerland as a base for his criminal activities because it was a rich country and an ideal target for international criminals of his calibre. He also thought he would be out of the reach of Interpol in Switzerland. It was this simple mistake which finally brought him into the wide net of the international police organization.

The French police system

The British police system is unusual in being based on local control, for the pattern in most of Europe is that of national police forces responsible to central government. France has four major police organizations, the Sûreté-Nationale being the most well known. This is a civil police force with headquarters in Paris which is answerable to the Minister of the Interior. The Sûreté is responsible for maintaining law and order and providing the specialized services required for this purpose. It operates throughout France and has detection flying squads (Brigade Mobile) based in the larger provincial towns. The other police organizations in the country are a municipal force which functions in rural France, the Gendarmerie Nationale, an armed force responsible to the Minister of Defence, and the Paris Préfecture of Police.

Above: *In France, unlike the UK or the USA, it is normal to use the criminal in a reconstruction of the crime. Here, the murder of a Gendarme, Neufcourt, is re-enacted in 1950. Standing by the car is the man accused of taking part.*

The Paris police

Paris had its own police in 1800 largely due to the traditional interest of the French kings in the security of the capital. Like London, the French capital city had its street crime and with criminal investigation appearing ineffective, the Prefect of Police took an unusual step – he called in an escaped convict to help. Eugène-François Vidocq (1775-1857) was an unusual man whom the authorities had failed to keep in prison following his conviction for minor crimes. Vidocq's knowledge of criminal affairs was such that the detective squad which he formed to assist the police met with immediate success.

Like Henry Fielding's Bow Street Runners, this squad of detectives proved to be a force to which the street criminals readily succumbed. In 1811, Vidocq was appointed Head of the Sûreté, a position which he held until 1827 when he resigned. He served in that capacity again for a short time in 1832 and subsequently became one of the first private detectives. The former convict proved to be a pioneer in criminal investigation.

The Sûreté today is headed by a Director-General and is organized in four directorates covering counter-espionage, criminal investigation, special branch and public security. It has 17 regional headquarters throughout France whose chief officers report to the Director-General. The roles of the counter-espionage directorate and Special Branch (Brigade Spéciale) are concerned with the security of the state against treason and insurrection.

The Special Branch, a squad of specially-selected detectives, gathers intelligence for the Ministry of the Interior and also supervises betting and gaming activities. The public security function is carried out by the uniformed branch of the police service operating routine patrols, traffic regulation and communications networks.

In 1951, a special force was set up under the Director-General of the Sûreté to coordinate police action in dealing with public disturbances occasioned by strikes or emergencies. This is the Republic Security Companies (CRS) which gained a certain notoriety for meting out rough treatment in quelling riotous student behaviour in the 1960s. There are sixty CRS units stationed throughout France and a local authority can request their assistance through the head of the Sûreté. As a matter of routine, CRS officers also carry out port and frontier security duties.

The French Sûreté

The criminal investigation branch of the Sûreté is similar in many respects to Scotland Yard. It operates a detective force known as the Police Judiciaire and maintains a criminal records office, fingerprint bureau and a forensic science laboratory. The early practice of criminal investigation in France was much influenced by the anthropometric system of identification developed by Alphonse Bertillon (1883-1914) who began his career as a clerk in the Paris Préfecture of Police. Although his system of identification by body measurement was overthrown by fingerprints, he is regarded as the founder of forensic photography which he pioneered in Paris.

U.S. police organization

The USA has the most diverse police organization in the world with as many as 40,000 individual and independent units of various sizes operating across the country. Police administration echoes the pattern of civil government and the jurisdiction of this large number of law enforcement units is variously federal, state and local. This diversity made nationwide law enforcement difficult as wanted criminals simply crossed state lines into a different area of police jurisdiction. With this in mind, Congress established the Bureau of Investigation in 1908 to provide the Department of Justice with a permanent crime investigation agency.

J. Edgar Hoover and the FBI

The early years of the Bureau's existence were not particularly distinguished owing to its restricted powers, but it was well placed for development when in 1924 the Attorney General appointed J. Edgar Hoover (1895-1972) to the position of

Below: *J. Edgar Hoover, Director of the FBI for nearly 50 years, photographed in the 1930s.*

Director. One of his first acts was to raise the standard of recruitment and from then on all agents were to be either qualified lawyers or accountants. They were dubbed G-men or 'government men'. Also in 1924, the bureau established an Identification Division with a nucleus of 800,000 fingerprints which under Hoover's direction has become the world's greatest fingerprint collection.

During the years between the two world wars, Hoover's men excelled themselves in dealing with prohibition and gang warfare and won extra powers from Congress for the fight against crime. Kidnapping was one of many criminal activities which became the province of the bureau in 1932 following the Lindbergh case which shocked the nation. In 1935 the bureau was given the appellation, Federal Bureau of Investigation (FBI), by which it is universally known today. By 1949 the FBI Director was able to state that of 261 cases of kidnapping dealt with by his agents, only two remained unsolved. Such was the success of the FBI that in 1939 the U.S. President gave it responsibility for all internal security matters including counter-espionage and anti-sabotage measures.

Today, police jurisdiction at a national level in the USA is carried out entirely by the FBI. The bureau provides central services for all identification, technical, forensic and statistical requirements. It also plays a major role in training police personnel through the National Police Academy which was set up in 1935. The FBI has an impressive record of achievement in police science and has been at the forefront of developing new ideas.

Probably the U.S. police at all levels are the best provided for in terms of equipment, technical facilities and communications. Considerable value is placed on crime scene investigation (CSI), for example, and many forces operate CSI units with specially-trained officers using custom-built vehicles equipped for evidence gathering. The aim is to secure physical evidence in the best condition to aid the crime laboratory.

The central crime laboratory

The FBI runs a central crime laboratory at its headquarters in Washington, DC and its resources are available to any police force. The most up-to-date and highly sophisticated technical facilities are thereby available to the smallest police force. Many large police departments have their own forensic science laboratories and in every respect U.S. police work is closely related to the 'lab'. The FBI's crime laboratory carries out upwards of 150,000 investigations a year on evidence material. New technology is rapidly transforming the nature and accuracy of laboratory work, and forensic examiners can now take latent fingerprints from the inside of gloves using lasers, or distinguish gender from a single strand of human hair. Most revolutionary of all, in the 1990s, has been the application of DNA profiling in providing virtually foolproof confirmation of identity from microscopic or degraded samples of human biological material.

U.S. crime levels

Criticism over political assassinations and the use of electronic surveillance methods have combined with an increase in U.S. crime figures to put the FBI under pressure. The 1990s have seen a huge increase in narcotics offences plus an alarming – and often related – surge in murder rates, notably in Miami and Washington, DC. The attempted assassination of President Ronald Reagan and the bloody Waco, Texas siege in 1993 involving 'Branch Davidian' cultist David Koresh and his followers helped renew arguments about the constitutional right to bear arms. This led to the introduction of limited federal firearms control legislation with the passing of the Brady Bill on 30 November 1993 in the teeth of fierce opposition from lobbyists including the powerful National Rifle Association.

International crime

The international character of much of today's crime – terrorism, fraud and drug trafficking – bears out the need for an international police organization. It was apparent as early as 1914 that the variety and speed of transportation available to the criminal needed to be matched by international cooperation between the world's police forces. Meeting in Monaco, delegates to the first interna-

Top: *Arthur Koehler, a wood technologist, examines the ladder used in the kidnapping of Charles Lindbergh's baby. He was able to match the grooves and nail holes in the ladder to the tools owned by Bruno Hauptmann (below) who had worked for the lumber firm that Koehler had painstakingly identified as the supplier of the wood which was used in the manufacture of the ladder. This evidence led to the execution of Hauptmann for the murder of the baby.*

'I HAVEN'T FALLEN OFF THE CHRISTMAS TREE'
The Yorkshire Ripper hunt

The multiple murderer strikes fear in us all. Somehow, it is possible to empathize with someone who commits a homicide, in a moment of frenzy, perhaps. But one killing after another? The imagination boggles.

The Yorkshireman who killed 13 women in a distinctively brutal manner was at large for over five years in the north of England. Such was the ferocity of his assaults on his victims that he was inevitably compared with the Victorian sex killer, Jack the Ripper. As time passed, and the macabre murders continued, the West Yorkshire Metropolitan Police found the pressure mounting.

Women were afraid to go outdoors after dark; questions were tabled in Parliament by anxious MPs. Certainly, every resource of local police organization was stretched to full capacity. As nerves frayed under constant media criticism, the hunt continued. Yet how could one man evade one of the biggest dragnets ever constructed?

The actual 'catch' was an oddly routine affair. But routine is important. By investigating how and why errors are made the system of police organization is gradually improved. Yet, much as we would like to imagine the smooth efficiency of computers and card indexes clicking into motion, there is always a fascinating, random element in a case such as this.

Perhaps, in some crazed way, Peter Sutcliffe did possess some form of psychotic genius — if only in his ability to lie his way successfully through several police interviews. He certainly had more than his share of what can be normally considered to be average good luck.

His trial opened in May 1981, and attracted worldwide press coverage.

"When you speak to God it's called praying; but when God speaks to you it's called schizophrenia." Thus did a West German observer comment on the psychiatric evidence given during the proceedings. Sutcliffe, who said he had heard the voice of God instructing him to kill and who claimed that his "latent genius if unleashed would rock the nation", was sentenced to life imprisonment for the murder of 13 women. The capture of the 34-year old ex altar-boy and grave-digger followed a trail of death and mutilation.

The first murder occurred in Leeds in October 1975 and the last in the same city in November 1980. In between, the Yorkshire Ripper killed 11 other women in Huddersfield, Halifax and Manchester and attacked seven others. His hunting grounds were the red-light districts of those towns where prostitutes made easy prey. He prowled around in his car until he fixed his target and,

•FO

following the routine bargaining for sex, felled her with a severe blow to the head delivered with a ballpeen hammer. He then set about his fiendish work with a knife, performing a ritualistic disfigurement of the body.

Sutcliffe was to say later that it was a miracle the police did not catch him earlier. He slipped in and out of police surveillance, enjoying the luck of the devil and building up a barrage of criticism which would later be levelled at the police. A £5 note was found in Jean Jordan's handbag after her murder in Manchester in October 1977. In the belief that she had been given the money by the killer, the police set about tracing the note. Banknote number AW 51121565 had been issued by the Midland Bank at Shipley on 27 September, a few days before the murder. It was part of a batch of £50,000 worth of notes which had been drawn by local firms to pay wages. The bank provided a list of firms who had received notes from this batch but there was no record of serial numbers that could be matched to individual withdrawals. Consequently, the police visited each company and interviewed its employees. Sutcliffe's firm was one of these and he was one of 8,300 men interviewed. His answers proved satisfactory and the heat was off.

Between March 1978 and June 1979, the police received several communications purporting to come "from the Ripper". There were three letters, two of which were sent directly to the police, and one received via a newspaper. The letters contained haunting phrases from the original Jack the Ripper letters sent to the authorities in 1888, but what seemed significant was the inclusion of details of the murder of Joan Harrison (Preston, November 1975) which had not been published.

Moreover, semen found on that victim's body was from a secretor with B-group blood, a combination found in only 6% of the population. This tied in with the sender of the letters, for the stamps had been moistened by the tongue of a secretor with B-group blood. The other communication received by the police was the tape, beginning "I'm Jack", which taunted them in a voice with a Wearside accent. This too had been sent in an envelope the flap of which had been moistened by a B-group secretor.

The police launched Project R, a massive publicity campaign unique to British criminal investigation. The "I'm Jack" tape was played in hundreds of clubs and pubs and broadcast on radio and TV. Samples of handwriting from the letters were published by the press and huge poster hoardings appeared in Leeds and elsewhere urging people to HELP US STOP THE RIPPER FROM KILLING AGAIN – LOOK AT HIS HANDWRITING, LISTEN TO HIS VOICE. In addition, photofit pictures and artists' impressions made up from descriptions given by women fortunate enough to have survived the Ripper's assaults were widely publicized. All this activity proved fruitless and the police were later criticized for misleading themselves

Above: *Peter Sutcliffe with his wife Sonia on their wedding day in 1974. She claimed she had no knowledge of his killings, and was determined to stick by him.*

over the tape. As events turned out, the Yorkshire Ripper had B-group blood but he was a non-secretor and therefore did not send the letters or tape.

On 2 January 1981, Sergeant Robert Ring and PC Robert Hydes set out on a routine panda car patrol in Sheffield. Driving along Melbourne Avenue, they spotted a parked Rover car which they thought deserved attention. The occupants were a man who gave his name as Peter Williams and a young coloured woman. Sergeant Ring thought he recognized the girl as a prostitute. "Who's she?", he asked. "My girl friend." "What's her name?" "I don't know. I haven't known her all that long." "Who are you trying to kid?" said Ring, adding "I haven't fallen off the Christmas tree."

A radio call was put in to the police computer at Hendon asking for a check on the Rover's registration number. Within two minutes Ring was informed that the number belonged not to a Rover but to a Skoda. Close examination of the number plate revealed that it was held on by adhesive tape. The driver, who had wandered off a few yards saying he was "bursting for a pee", was driven with his companion to Hammerton Road police station for questioning. The following day, Sergeant Ring returned to the scene and found a hammer and a knife which Williams, alias Peter William Sutcliffe, the Yorkshire Ripper, had hidden while ostensibly relieving himself.

The search for the mass murderer had ended but behind the jubilation of the police lurked the shadow of public criticism. Why, it was asked, with all their manpower and scientific resources, had the police let their man slip through nine different interviews and why did

The Judge praised the police. But do they deserve it? The case against them shows nothing but incompetence, stupidity and bureaucratic arrogance.

GREGORY : He expected criticism of police

HOBSON : Too little doubt over hoax

BIRDSALL : The detectives put him on file

OLDFIELD : The tape and letters obsessed him

Above: *Public criticism of Assistant Chief Constable Oldfield and Detective Chief Superintendent Hobson was strong. Although Chief Constable Gregory pointed to the difficulties of the case—too little public interest, random killings, no apparent motive—the fact remains that obsession with the Geordie tapes prevented earlier capture.*

they allow themselves to be misled over the "I'm Jack" tape?

One answer lies in the sheer magnitude of the task confronting any police force in tracking down the multiple murderer operating in different locations. In the course of their five-year investigation, which cost four million pounds, the police checked 5.2 million car registration numbers, interviewed 250,000 individuals and took 32,000 written statements. At the peak of the investigation, 250 detectives worked full-time checking every piece of information that came into their hands, including over a thousand letters a day. The police admitted making mistakes but their defence lay in the fact that they *ultimately* got their man. Despite all their previous errors, they still managed to overcome the Ripper's self-confessed 'latent genius' by alert policing plus the central computer. And, we might add, with an element of something that had so far been wholly on Peter Sutcliffe's side — sheer good luck!

Below: *Every communication had to be examined. This note, thought to be the Ripper's work, appears to deny the murder of Barbara Leach in Bradford 1979. The police believed her to be his twelfth victim.*

` clueless `

POOR OLD OLDFIELD
WORKED IN A COLDFIELD

HOBSON HAS NO CHOICE
MISLED BY A VOICE

RELEASE OF DRURY
AROUSES FURY

BRADFORD WAS NOT ME
BUT JUST WAIT AND SEE

SHEFFIELD WILL NOT BE MISSED
NEXT ON THE LIST
` The Streetcleaner `
(T.S.)

1279

tional criminal police congress decided to establish an organization for this purpose.

World War One prevented this coming to immediate fruition but in 1923 at Vienna, the International Criminal Police Commission (ICPC) was created. World War Two hampered progress so that it was not until 1946 that the ICPC, or Interpol as it was to become known, really came into its own. In that year, under the presidency of Monsieur F.E. Louwage, Inspector-General of the Belgian Police, Interpol became established with a headquarters office in Paris in the building occupied by the Sûreté-Nationale.

Interpol

The purpose of Interpol is to coordinate efforts against international crime by promoting mutual assistance between criminal police authorities in different countries. It was set out clearly that this objective was to be achieved within the limits of individual members' legal systems and excluded political, religious, military or racial activities.

Interpol is not a world police force but a coordinating centre for information enabling its member countries to track crime beyond national boundaries. It works by exchanging information and by identifying and securing the apprehension of wanted individuals and suspects.

Interpol rightly prides itself on the quality of its communications, an essential ingredient in international criminal investigation. Its radio-communications centre in Lyons is equipped with powerful transmitters which maintain contact with 20 regional radio stations covering Europe, the Middle East, North Africa, North and South America and the Far East. Interpol staff, working in English, French and Spanish, deal with a large flow of information and enquiries, drawing on a huge data base which carries information on top criminals and records of passports, car registrations, stolen property and missing persons.

Below: *Police investigation room. Electronic technology plays an increasingly important part in the fight against crime.*

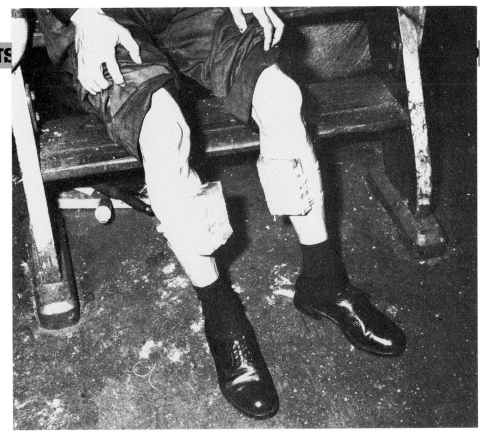

RENSIC • FORENSIC • FO

Left: *Narcotics are tied onto a sailor's legs in an attempt to smuggle them into Hong Kong. In the 1990s, dealing in drugs has become a massive business, and Hong Kong, easily accessible to the 'Golden Triangle', is one of the world's exchange centres of narcotics, besides having a serious drug problem itself.*

Interpol goes hi-tech

Following its relocation to Lyons in 1989, Interpol stepped into the technological age. Gone are the long rooms of card indexes and files, replaced by a powerful computer system able to retrieve comprehensive data on four million known criminals worldwide at the touch of a button – and instantly accessible to the organization's 174 global members. A new Criminal Intelligence Unit offers a computer graphics facility – used in a 1993 fraud inquiry to trace connections among 16,000 bank accounts.

National Central Bureaux

Each member country has a National Central Bureaux, for example the FBI in Washington, DC or Scotland Yard in London, which sends information of international interest to Interpol HQ and undertakes such police operations as the law permits to make searches and arrests at the request of another country. Interpol publishes an official journal, *International Criminal Police Review*, to disseminate information among its members and also seeks agreement through international agencies such as the UN on drug control and extradition procedures. In this way, over 170 member coun-

tries are better informed in their fight against international fraud, drug trafficking and counterfeit operations.

Narcotics control

Drug trafficking is big international business and nearly a third of the enquiries dealt with by Interpol concern drug offences. The rapid growth of heroin, cocaine and crack addiction among the younger age groups of the western nations has resulted in a massive growth in violent street crime, which is taxing the resources and detection skills of all police organizations. The New York Police Department estimates that there are at least some 300,000 heroin users in the city. Smuggling the drugs to satisfy this appetite is big business to the tune of billions of dollars a year for the dealers. Raw heroin is imported from the 'Golden Triangle' of Thailand, Burma and Laos and from Mexico, Central and South America.

The U.S. Bureau of Narcotics, which has been a part of the Drug Enforcement Agency since the early 1970s, works closely with Interpol to plot the movements of known drug traffickers and to monitor their supply routes. National bureaux in France, Italy, Turkey and Holland as well as the

Above: *FBI forensic examiners analyse samples for traces of illegal narcotics. The continued rise in drug-related crime provides a growing source of work for the laboratories.*

Far East and South America have cooperated fully in an international strategy to tackle the illicit drug trade at source by raiding heroin factories. Billions of dollars worth of hard drugs are seized every year following this kind of often painstaking and hazardous surveillance. However, this is a field of highly organized criminal endeavour that is so hugely lucrative, it is fast becoming the single most important police activity worldwide – surpassing even international terrorism as a top priority in the 1990s.

There is little doubt that without the benefit of coordinating agencies such as Interpol and the DEA, the world's crime problems in general, and narcotics violations in particular, would be even worse than they are. One unfortunate consequence of successful police and customs activity is that any shortage in supply leads to higher prices and more demand from the drug cartels – who see themselves as having a no-lose position. Nevertheless, police methods have come a long way since Fielding's day – but his concept of rapid communications as the key to crime investigation is even more valid in today's fast-moving society.

WITCH-HUNT

During early colonial days in America all but a very few men believed in the actual existence of demons and witches and harbored many superstitions that had been handed down from the Middle Ages ——

TODAY most people laughingly dismiss witchcraft as a superstition of the ignorant. But in seventeenth-century Europe and America, witches, defined by the English judge Lord Coke as persons who had "conference with the Devil to consult with him or to do some act," were taken very seriously. Witches were women—the male equivalent was warlock—and as a result of their dealings with the Devil were commonly believed to be able to perform supernatural acts.

AROUND THE WORLD, witch-hunting was a major occupation. A 1647 woodcut (left) shows British witch-finder Matthew Hopkins. In America, several women were hanged at Gallows Hill, Salem (below). But Tituba (far right) never faced trial because she repented.

The penalty for being proved a witch was death, and in the few years of Oliver Cromwell's rule in England many unfortunates accused of witchcraft perished on the gallows—60 being hanged in a single year in Suffolk, a county which the notorious witch-hunter Matthew Hopkins pronounced to be infested with witches.

The panic on the subject was the natural result of Puritanical teaching acting on the mind and predisposing the ruling authorities to see Satanic influences at work in the community, expressed through the supernatural phenomena of witchcraft.

The seeds of the superstition crossed the Atlantic with the Pilgrim Fathers, and at a time when it was beginning to disappear in England it flourished alarmingly in the state of Massachusetts—which in 1692 was the scene of the most celebrated witch-hunt and witch trials in history. It all happened in the small rural community of Salem Village, since renamed Danvers, situated near the old port of Salem a few miles to the northeast of Boston.

The Rev. Samuel Parris, a local preacher, had previously been engaged in trade in the West Indies before accepting a call to the parish of Salem Village. He

had brought back a married couple with him from Barbados, slaves called John and Tituba, whose presence undoubtedly lent prestige to the parsonage. Tituba, who was half Carib and half black, spent a good deal of time with the two children in the household, the Parris' nine-year-old daughter Betty, and her cousin Abigail Williams, who was two years older.

During the winter of 1691-92, a group of eight girls, including Abigail and Betty, mostly teen-aged, used to meet in the kitchen premises of the minister's house in the company of Tituba. It was later assumed that Tituba had stuffed their impressionable heads with tales of African or West Indian magic, and had even practised it with them—although no credible evidence of this came to light in the subsequent trials which were documented in great detail.

Tituba's activities do not seem to have gone beyond fortune telling and possibly what another New England divine, the Rev. Cotton Mather—who had made a

Mary Evans

study of witchcraft and written a book about it—described as "little sorceries" practised with sieve and scissors and candle.

These sessions ended by driving Betty, Abigail, and a 12-year-old girl named Ann Putnam into what was evidently a hysterical illness. Abigail and Ann, in particular, moaned and shrieked for no apparent reason, grovelling and writhing on the ground and occasionally acting as if they believed that they had been transformed into animals.

The symptoms soon spread throughout the child population in Salem Village, and as a result it was concluded by the adult community—led by Parris and other clergymen in the area—that the girls were bewitched. Eventually, in February 1692, Abigail and Ann were able to name three of their tormentors. The first of these was Tituba; the other two were an elderly pipe-smoking hag named Sarah Good, and a moderately well-to-do married woman named Sarah Osburne, who owned some property.

The two Sarahs seem to have been unpopular in the settlement and were certainly disapproved of by the Puritan leaders of the community—Sarah Good, because she had become something of a tramp who begged from door to door, and furthermore did not go to church, and Sarah Osburne, because as a widow she lived in sin with her overseer before marrying him as her second husband.

The three women were now arrested and brought before two magistrates, John Hathorne and Jonathan Corwin, who were sent out from Salem Village to examine the accused in a public session at one of the local churches which had been borrowed for the purpose. Both the Sarahs denied everything. Asked why she did not attend church, Sarah Good replied

that she had no suitable clothes. Further questioned as to what she said when she went away muttering from people's houses, she answered confidently: "It is the commandments I say. I may say my commandments, I hope."

As for the unfortunate Sarah Osburne, she had been dragged from her sickbed and had to be supported by two constables during her interrogation. She was obviously very ill, and the most the magistrates could get out of her was that she was "more like to be bewitched than that she should be a witch."

After the two Sarahs had been taken off again to prison, the extraordinary Tituba was brought in. She produced an imaginative confession in which she said just the kind of thing her Puritan accusers wished her to say. She talked about red cats and red rats. These cats and rats, she declared, could talk to her and in fact had said to her: "Serve me." She went on to tell of "a Thing" which she could only describe as "something like a cat"—it had a woman's face and it had wings, and it was Gammer Osburne's creature. These and other shapes, she said, told her to pinch Betty and Abigail, but "I would not hurt Betty—I loved Betty." They also told her to attack Ann Putnam with a knife. Ann and Abigail were then fetched into court in Tituba's presence and they began to moan and whimper.

"Who hurts the children now?" asked magistrate Hathorne.

"I am blind now," Tituba cunningly answered. "I cannot see." Thus the slave made it clear that second sight was not for a witch who had repented and renounced her calling.

No doubt Tituba's confession saved her life, and she was never arraigned. Meanwhile the list of suspect witches quickly grew, largely on the accusation of Abigail and Ann—though other girls occasionally joined in, and some of the accused followed Tituba's example by confessing.

It is noteworthy that none of those who confessed and implicated others was executed. Only those who steadfastly protested their innocence in the event suffered. Among those in this category were George Burroughs, a minister of religion, Martha Corey, who was a church member in good standing, and Rebecca Nurse, an invalid of unsullied reputation.

Not even children escaped, since Dorcas Good, the five-year-old daughter of the pipe-smoking Sarah, was also hauled off to prison.

There were also a few old villagers —such as the tavern keeper Bridget Bishop and Susanna Martin—who had been suspected of witchcraft in the past, and they were likewise taken into custody.

The Governor of Massachusetts, Sir

William Phips, appointed a special commission of seven judges, presided over by the Governor's Deputy, Chief Justice William Stoughton, to sit in Salem Village and try the suspects. It might be expected that the two Sarahs would be tried first, but this was not possible. Sarah Osburne died in prison before she could be brought into court again, while Sarah Good's case was put back until the delivery of her child—since she was pregnant at the time of her arrest.

Consequently the first to face a formal trial was Bridget Bishop, against whom there was already considerable local prejudice. Not only had she been suspected of practising sorcery in the past, but she was regarded as a flashy dresser and an unsatisfactory tavern keeper.

Her "red paragon bodice" set her style, as did her "smooth and flattering manner" with men, and it was a long standing complaint that she permitted young people to loiter at unseemly hours in her tavern, playing at "shovel-board" and disturbing the sleep of decent neighbours.

Her trial, like that of most of the others, was a travesty of justice, since the record of the pre-trial examination before the magistrates was accepted by the court as consisting of proven facts, rather than something to be tested. In the words of Cotton Mather, describing the court procedure in Bridget's case, "there was little occasion to prove the witchcraft, this being evident and notorious to all beholders."

Poor Bridget, who like all the other

HER CRIME was probably running a rowdy tavern. But Bridget Bishop was hanged as a witch on Gallows Hill (top). Sheriff Corwin reported back that she had been executed (below). Other Salem "witches" were to live.

June 10 = 1692.

According to the within written precept I have taken the body
of the within named Briget Bishop out of thair Majesty
Goal in Salem and safely conurayho her to the place from
for her Execution and Caused y d Briget to d haige
by the nek untill shoe was dead and buried in the place
all which was according to the time within Required and
So J make Rehurne by m — George Corwin Sherif

defendants in the subsequent trials was denied the aid of defence counsel, got off to a bad start. While walking under guard from Salem prison to the court she cast a glance at "the great and spacious meeting-house", and at once a great clatter arose within. Those sent to see what the woman's evil eye had done reported that "they found a board which was strongly fastened with several nails transported to another quarter of the house."

Four male witnesses testified that she haunted their beds at night, sometimes coming in her own form, sometimes like a black pig and in one instance with the body of a monkey, the feet of a cock, and the face of a man. Three children of these witnesses pined away and died, they swore, because being good men they had virtuously repelled her advances.

Testimony to the effect that Bridget's own husband thought she was a witch was given by a female witness named Elizabeth Balch, who described how she had once seen a quarrel between them. Bridget was riding pillion on horseback behind her husband when the latter spurred his horse to a pace that nearly threw her. Bridget thereupon lost her temper, and they had words. She was a "bad wife", said her husband; "the Devil had come bodily to her . . . and she sat up all night with the Devil." What particularly struck Mistress Balch, who was riding beside them, was that throughout this tirade Bridget did not once open her mouth to defend herself.

Other witnesses, who had searched Bridget's house in Salem, found in the cellar some dolls made of rags and hog's bristles, into which pins had been stuck. When she was confronted with these objects, Bridget could give the court no "reasonable and tolerable" explanation.

Both immediately before her trial and immediately afterwards, Bridget was physically examined for witch marks by a jury of matrons—who were equipped with pins which they stuck into any part of her body that looked at all unusual. On the first occasion the women discovered a "witch's tet" between "ye pudendum and anus"; on the second, three hours later, this "tet" had withered to dry skin.

DEATH WAS THE USUAL PENALTY FOR WITCHCRAFT IN THOSE DAYS, AND THE CONDEMNED PERSONS WERE SENT TO THE GALLOWS. —

The court jury found Bridget Bishop guilty and the judges condemned her to death. Ten days elapsed before the sentence could be carried out, since it had to be legalized by reviving an old colonial law which made witchcraft a capital offence. Then on June 10, 1692, High Sheriff George Corwin took Bridget to the top of Gallows Hill and hanged her from the branches of a great oak tree.

The court did not sit again for nearly a month. The reason for the delay, which was kept from the public, was a difference which occurred among the judges as to the credence to be given to spectral evidence. At least one member of the commission was impressed by the fact that, had such evidence been held inadmissible, Bridget Bishop would have been convicted for little more than wearing scarlet, countenancing "shovel-board" in her tavern and getting herself talked about—no doubt all offences, but hardly capital ones even in those harsh days.

Since witchcraft involved theological as well as legal considerations, Governor Phips referred the question to a committee of 12 ministers of religion in the Boston region. Unfortunately the committee, to which the historian Cotton Mather acted as secretary, equivocated. While advising that conviction should in future be based on evidence "certainly more considerable than barely the accused person being represented by a spectre unto the afflicted", at the same time it praised the "sedulous and assiduous endeavours" of the magistrates and judges who had in practice disregarded nearly all other evidence.

The committee went on to "humbly recommend the speedy and vigorous prosecution of such as have rendered themselves obnoxious."

First to be tried was Rebecca Nurse, an old invalid lady, almost totally deaf. The jury had before them a petition signed by more than a score of respectable inhabitants of Salem Village, testifying to her unwitchlike character, piety and the extraordinary care she had lavished on the Christian upbringing of her children.

"I am innocent and clear and have not been able to get out of doors these eight or nine days," Rebecca protested. "I never afflicted no child, no, never in my life."

One of the witnesses against Rebecca was a certain Deliverance Hobbs, who had herself confessed to being a witch and repented with the result that her life was spared. When Deliverance came into court, Rebecca was said to have turned her head towards her and exclaimed: "What, do you bring her? She is one of us."

However, after deliberating on these matters, the jury brought in a verdict of not guilty. Ann Putnam, Abigail Williams, and several other girls were in the court house, and they immediately set up a howling and wailing, twisting their bodies as if convulsed.

When the din had subsided somewhat, Chief Justice Stoughton addressed the jurors. "I will not impose on the jury," he said, "but I must ask you if you considered one statement made by the prisoner." The judge then repeated what the accused was alleged to have said to Deliverance Hobbs. "Has the jury weighed the implications of this statement?"

Neither the foreman nor the other jurors could remember exactly what Rebecca had said. Rebecca was thereupon questioned again and asked to explain herself.

THEY LIVED and died here . . . Salem, the New England village where Puritans held their famous trial of witches.

The Bettmann Archive

Unfortunately Rebecca, as she herself put it afterwards, was "something hard of hearing and full of grief", and consequently did not give a very satisfactory answer. The jury again retired and this time brought in a verdict of guilty.

On trial with Rebecca Nurse were Susanna Martin, the pipe-smoking Sarah Good, and two other women who had been denounced as witches, Elizabeth How and Sarah Wild, the latter by the nefarious Abigail Hobbs and the former by a family named Perley from Ipswich who claimed that their ten-year-old daughter had been "afflicted" by Goody How. "Did I hurt you?" asked Elizabeth How, when she was confronted with the child and took her hand. "No, never!" the little girl replied. "If I did complain of you in my fits, I knew not that I did so."

The tale of Susanna Martin's spectral misdeeds was recited at length. A neighbouring farmer swore that she had cast a spell upon his herd of oxen because he refused to hitch his ox cart to haul her some staves. "Your oxen will never do you much service!" Susanna was alleged to have said, with the result that the oxen took fright and plunged into the sea.

Another neighbour told an unlikely tale of a phantom puppy which sprang at his throat as a result of Susanna's witcheries. Like Bridget Bishop, Susanna was also said to have molested honest men in their bedchambers, "scrabbling at the window", hopping down from the sill and boldly getting into bed.

All four women were found guilty, and along with Rebecca Nurse, they were hanged on Gallows Hill.

Four men were condemned in the immediately following trial. They included the Rev. George Burroughs who was charged with seducing girls to witchcraft by offering them "fine cloathes" and subsequently biting them. The girls had toothmarks all over their arms and Burrough's mouth was prized open when it was established to the satisfaction of the jury that his teeth were responsible for the marks.

FIGHTING for her life . . . a woman accused of witchcraft faces the court in Salem. But eventually, the hysteria that swept the village was to die down.

Then there was the case of the octogenarian Giles Cory who had incriminated his wife Martha—though his testimony had amounted to little more than an expression of wonder that Martha should linger by the fire to pray long after he expected her in bed, and one of annoyance that when the examinations were going on before the magistrates she had hidden his saddle to prevent him from riding to court. ("Nevertheless," she commented later, "he went for all that.")

In due course he, too, was arrested and charged with witchcraft—having apparently been denounced by some of the girls in their fits. However, when brought to court he remained more or less speechless and steadfastly refused to plead to the indictment. "I am a poor man and cannot help it" was all he would say.

Under English criminal procedure, an accused person who "stood mute" and refused to plead was subjected to *peine forte et dure*—in other words he was tied to the floor of his cell and heavy weights were placed on his chest until he consented to plead "guilty" or "not guilty".

The result was that Giles Cory was pressed to death by the sheriff in an open

Mary Evans

field beside the jail. His only recorded utterance as rock after rock was piled on his chest was to cry out "More Weight!" Such a revolting punishment was never afterwards carried out in America.

Although only 19 people in addition to Giles Cory were executed for witchcraft in Salem in 1692—a number small by contemporary European standards—nevertheless about 400 people were arrested and crammed into the local jails. Others fled to the safety of other states, abandoning their property and livelihood. However, a reaction set in quickly and the popular hysteria died down as suddenly as it had begun.

In October 1692, Governor Phips cancelled the special commission and re-manded the prisoners in custody on witch-craft charges to the ordinary courts, which acquitted the majority. The rest were pardoned.

Afterwards all concerned with the witch-hunt sought to make amends as best they could. A day was set aside for public mourning and prayers for forgiveness. "We walked in clouds and could not see our way," declared the Rev. John Hale, who had testified against Bridget Bishop. "And we have most cause to be humbled for error . . . which cannot be retrieved." Judges and juries made public repentance, expressing their "deep sense of sorrow" to the survivors of their victims and their heirs.

No execution for witchcraft ever again

ARRESTED . . . The witch-hunters swoop on yet another woman as the purge goes on. But after the Salem trials, no witch was to be executed in America.

took place in Colonial America. Sanity gradually prevailed in place of madness, and the spirit of enlightenment and rationalism eventually triumphed over ignorance and superstition—though not entirely. Ideological witch-hunts still occurred in the United States right up until the mid-1950 s. They were carried out with Puritan zeal by such campaigners as Anthony Comstock, secretary of the Society for Suppression of Vice, and the late Senator Joseph McCarthy and his un-American activities committee.

SHOOT-OUT IN CISCO

Dressing up as Santa Claus sounded like a bright idea to four young stick-up men bent on robbing the Cisco branch of First National City Bank. But the ploy turned out to be a total fiasco which ended on a makeshift noose.

CHILDREN in the United States were shocked and bewildered, that January day in 1929, when they learned from the excited chatter of their parents that this was the day that Santa Claus would go on trial.

There was hardly an American home, within reach of newspapers or earshot of radios, in which the name Santa Claus was not the central topic of conversation. But, to add to the concern of the younger generation, it was a name uttered with distaste and hostility. For it seemed that the world had been turned upside down, and that the old gentleman in the red gown had suffered from some kind of 20th-century aberration and turned bank robber.

The facts were every bit as bizarre as childish imaginings could make them. Arraigned at that very moment in a courtroom in Eastland, Texas, was a 24-year-old, good-looking hoodlum named Marshall Ratliff, who had led a gang of bandits into the First National Bank, in the small Texas town of Cisco, the day before Christmas Eve—dressed as Santa Claus.

But to District Attorney J. Frank Sparks, striding purposefully into the courtroom, there was more to the case against Ratliff than impudent mockery of the festive season. For, in the course of the ludicrous Santa Claus charade, three men, two of them policemen, had died. A charge of murder was to be laid against "Santa" Ratliff, but first, that morning of January 23, he faced a Texan jury on an indictment of armed robbery.

The old redstone building of the East-land County courthouse was packed, and the gossip of the tensed-up spectators ceased immediately as a side door opened and in walked the young Santa in a smart brown suit with matching shirt and tie. With tight-shut lips and carefully watching eyes, he looked more like a know-all, worldly-wise and clever young man than the benign old character whose role he had assumed.

In truth, he was not what the period usually dubbed a "city slicker". He was, indeed, just one of Cisco's 8000 people and a score or so of his fellow townsmen—outraged at what he and his gang had done to their quiet little American backwater—had squeezed into the public seats. Many of them were consumed not only with anger, but with indignation that such a boy should have brought such shame on that nice mother of his who ran a "respectable" and popular café in their town.

Judge G. L. Davenport took his seat on the bench, and District Attorney Sparks called his first, and crucial, witness, Alex Spears—son-in-law of the First National's president, who had served in the bank as cashier on the day of the hold-up. Sparks told his dramatic story tersely, but with small remembered details which immediately conveyed to the jury the strong impression which the events had made upon him.

Hypnotized

"It was just around noon when Santa Claus came in followed by three other men. I said 'Hello, Santa Claus' but he refused to answer. I twice asked him how he was and then finally he just grunted. He went to the cage of Jewell Poe, the only teller on duty, took his pistol and stuck it in his suit. Then one of the other men stepped up to Joe, pulled out two pistols and said 'Stick 'em up!' Then I realized this was a hold-up."

Alex Spears expressed how everyone in the bank—himself, Jewell Poe, and the customers—had at first been unable to take in what was happening. Not unnaturally they were hypnotized by the sight of the crimson costume. Joe had smiled and asked "Santa" the obvious question: "What do you mean?" Spears looked earnestly at the jury to emphasize the astonishing answer that came from the supposed bringer of Christmas goodwill: "I mean business, big boy."

And what happened then, the D.A. demanded. Santa had flicked his wrist as an order to Poe to leave his cage, and told him: "Get that vault opened." Alex

SENSATION . . . The Cisco Daily News gave the hold-up front page coverage on the following day. Below: contemporary prints of Cisco's Main Street, where the gun battle took place; and bank premises.

TRANSFIXED and terrified by the sudden transformation in the benign figure of Santa Claus, these bank employees all witnessed the hold-up.

Spears recalled the next second vividly. "Jewell looked towards me and I said 'Go ahead'. Santa said something to the man holding the guns. I think it was 'Let's get it', and they went around behind the cage towards the vault."

Spears had set the scene but, as witness followed witness, the court heard of the extraordinary events that had gripped Cisco from that moment onwards. It heard, for instance, of how—at the moment the hold-up men were on their way to the vault—a Mrs. Blasengame entered the bank with her 6-year-old daughter, Frances. The eager little girl at once spotted Santa and, thinking that her dearest wish for a personal meeting was at last being granted, began dragging her mother towards him.

But Mrs. Blasengame, who had taken in more of the scene than her daughter, grasped at once what was happening. Hauling Frances by the hand she made for the rear door of the bank, gasping: "Oh, my Lord." Little Frances, understandably, put the wrong construction on the situation. As she was lifted off her feet by her mother she shrieked out, "They're gonna shoot Santa Claus!"

Other witnesses remembered that, as the mother and daughter disappeared into a back alley behind the bank, one of the gunmen snarled: "Come back here!" But, by that time, Mrs. Blasengame, with sobbing Frances still firmly in tow, was half-way to the adjoining police station, yelling: "They're robbing the bank! They're holding up the First National!"

Piece by piece, the gaping jury heard the subsequent story assembled into one

incredible narrative. The District Attorney and his witnesses told how the news had flashed around Cisco in a matter of minutes, and how almost every able-bodied man, it seemed, had rushed for his gun. Armed men hurried towards Avenue D, Cisco's main street and the site of the First National.

Soon, witnesses testified, there seemed to be shooting going on everywhere in the vicinity of the bank—both inside and outside. One hold-up man, the court was told, shouted, "It must be the police." And "Santa" bellowed back, "It must be every damn body in town!" No-one in the witness stand was clear about who was involved in the fracas, but the prosecution centred its attention on two: Police Chief Bit Bedford and Policeman George Carmichael. But the jury would not hear from them, the District Attorney said, for they had both died from gunshot wounds.

Focus of admiration

Franks then outlined the sequence of events that followed the outbreak of shooting. The stick-up men, he said, scooped up $12,000 in cash and another $150,000 in non-negotiable "paper", and made their way, heads down, to their waiting, stolen blue Buick sedan. With half the maddened town following on foot and firing, they drove away down Avenue D, making poor progress because the car was running out of gas.

At an intersection, the District Attorney testified, the thieves blocked the path of an oncoming car and ordered its occupants, a Christmas-shopping family, to hand it over to them. The family did so, but the quick-witted, 14-year-old son who was at the wheel had the sense to take the ignition key with him. As soon as they discovered that the gang switched back to the Buick and took off once more. They left behind a shot and dying comrade and worse still for them, the District Attorney drily reported, they left their loot behind. Their first action in switching cars had been to transfer the money and, when they reverted to the Buick, they had no time to retrieve it.

Carl Wylie, a 22-year-old oil driller, came to the witness-stand to take up the story. The heavy, husky young man was a focus of admiration in the court for he had personally, if unwillingly, spent some time in the company of the three remaining getaway bandits. As he explained, he had been hijacked at his father's farm as he returned from the oilfields after midnight in his new Dodge.

"One man walked over to me holding a pistol," Carl said, "and he told me, 'We're taking this car.'" Exactly as Alex Spears had done in the bank, Carl Wylie demanded: "What do you mean?" The gunman told him: "We mean get moving. Make this baby roll out of here!" Carl had done so and, at that moment, he caught a glimpse of his father running out from the porch of the family house with a shotgun in his hand.

Identification

Carl was hit in the left arm and cried out in pain, but he kept driving. "I said, 'Now where?' and one of the men said, 'Go north until I tell you different.'" Carl related how he drove on, his arm burning from the wound. Then Ratliff, who had long since abandoned his Santa Claus costume, became worried about the question of identification. For, Carl told the court, "He turned to me and asked, 'Do you know who we are?' I said, 'I think I do', and he said: 'Ain't you kind of scared to be with us?' I said, 'Yes, sir, I am. But I hope I can get this car back to my daddy in one piece. It ain't six months old.'"

So they drove on through the night and the next day, with Carl using his own money to buy gasoline. But every direction they took they came across distant signs of roadblocks and, constantly, they were doubling back. In the end, it was the practical Carl who took the initiative.

"I said to them," he testified, 'Fellows, I just don't see how you're going to make it. Every time you get on the highway you hit a roadblock, and when you get on those back roads you're sooner or later going to run into patrols. We seen an airplane already and come daylight I think that will be back. They'll look for you section at a time and they'll surround you tight, by the hour."

By now the stick-up men sensed that, as a man who moved in the same small-town world as themselves, Carl had probably identified them. He had. In addition to Ratliff, there were young

Robert Hill, in his twenties, and Henry Helms, who, at 32, was the oldest of the bank-robbing quartet. Although Carl did not know it then, the fourth gang member, Louis Davis, was the one who had been left behind in Cisco and died of his wounds.

Carl continued with his narrative. "Helms said, 'We'll die fighting if we're surrounded.' I said, 'Well, maybe you will, but I don't want to die with you.' Hill said, 'I think maybe we ought to let Carl go,' and Ratliff said, 'O.K., we'll turn Carl loose, but I think we better keep hold of this car.' I said, 'I've done everything just the way you wanted me to, so I think you ought to leave my car.'"

Openly cheerful

Astonishingly, the jury learned, they did just that. They found another vehicle and they told Carl Wylie that he was free to go—adding one proviso: "Don't tell 'em where we are." Carl replied: "I don't know where we are." Then, as the tail-light of the bank robbers' newly-acquired car disappeared, he drove on into the dawn and back into Cisco. At 5 a.m. he was in Cisco police station, reporting his remarkable experience.

By the time Carl Wylie stepped down from the witness-chair, "Santa" Ratliff was looking comfortably composed and at ease. The prosecution lawyers were well aware of the reason. For all the testimony that had been given, no-one had been able to say they had seen him using a gun during the hold-up. As the jury trooped out, he seemed set, at worst, for no more than a moderate jail term.

The verdict was not long in coming: guilty of armed robbery. Judge Davenport set the sentence at 99 years, and "Santa" now appeared openly cheerful—for it appeared to him, and to others in court, that he might well be at liberty again in five or six years—and, in any case, his destination was not to be the gas chamber.

But there were other events yet to be fed into the machinery of the law. In particular, there was the question of the murder of Cisco Police Chief Bit Bedford in the aftermath of the hold-up. So it was that, on March 26, "Santa" Ratliff was put on trial for that murder—this time in Abilene.

Once more, Ratliff was his confident, cocky self. He was obviously pleased to see so many young girls in the courtroom. From what they had heard, and the

AT THE COURTHOUSE soon after their capture, robbers Hill and Helms (ringed) pose with the posse which had tracked them down. Peace officers and volunteers from all over the region took part in the chase. It was a fine example of the American tradition of mutual help and cooperation between police and citizens.

Fort Worth Star-Telegram

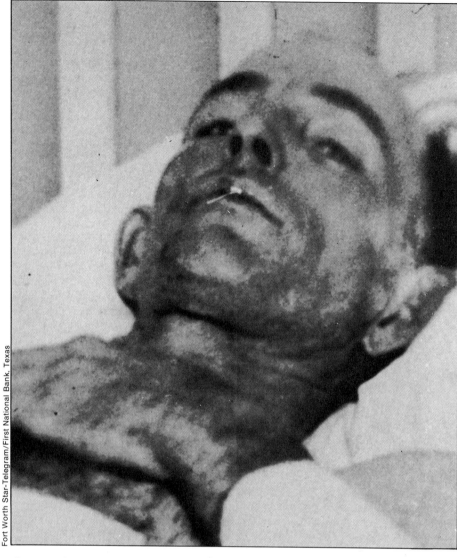

Fort Worth Star-Telegram/First National Bank, Texas

pictures they had studied in the newspapers, Santa was really very good-looking. They had come more to judge whether the rumour about his glamour was accurate than to listen to the proceedings.

For the most part, the evidence was a repeat of that which had been given to the court in Eastland—except that now the charge was far more dangerous for the prisoner. Ratliff entered court wearing a sober, black bow-tie, and one by one the Eastland witnesses came to the stand to repeat their stories—only this time their evidence sounded far more sinister. When the jury returned, after two hours of discussion, their verdict was apparent in their eyes even before it was read out to the court: guilty.

"Santa's" jaw sagged and he stared ahead with disbelief as the judge sentenced him to die in the electric chair. A ghost of a smile formed on his face, but vanished at once as his watching mother screamed out, "God, my boy! Oh, God, my boy!"

Ratliff's two surviving fellow Christ-

mas bandits had gone their way along the path of justice before him. Henry Helms was tried at Eastland on February 20, 1928, and Alex Spears, the bank cashier, again was called upon to recount the events of the hold-up. Others told of seeing George Carmichael, the policeman, fall fatally wounded. Witness after witness testified that Helms had fired two pistols at everyone crossing his path as the gang made their getaway.

When it came, the verdict of guilty was no surprise to the spectators, and Helms listened to the death sentence without emotion. The case of Robert Hill, the third surviving bandit, was quite different from the other two. He, too, was tried at Eastland, but he pleaded guilty and, as his attorney told the court: "He is ready to confess all his sins and take the consequences. He is a boy who never had a chance."

That was, indeed, the story that Hill told: father died while he was a baby, mother died soon afterwards, and the boy ended up in the care of institutions—one of them, because of some official care-

THE SHOOT-OUT in Cisco cost the life of first-time criminal Louis Davis (left). On leaving the bank the gang tried to take a girl (above) as hostage. (Right) some of the townsmen who joined in the chase through the streets of Cisco.

lessness, having been a reformatory even though he had committed no offence. Ratliff, he said, had planned the robbery and assured his gang that there would be no trouble. As they drove into Cisco on the fateful day they had sung hymns.

One thing that Hill's trial made abundantly clear was that there could not have been a more stupid ruse than Ratliff's dressing up as Santa. No one, Ratliff had told his men, would look suspiciously at Santa Claus entering a bank. But, as Hill had learned, *everyone* stopped to stare at Santa walking down the street.

The jury accepted Hill's decision to throw himself on the mercy of the court, and the foreman announced: "We find the defendant, Robert M. Hill, guilty as charged and assess his punishment at 99 years in the penitentiary." The state

First National Bank, Texas

aged. The howling mob broke into the jail and searched him out. "Come on out, Santa Claus," they screamed, brushing aside the few frightened guards who pleaded with them to go home. "Here he is," a woman screeched. "Here's Santa Claus —here's Santa, the beast!" The prisoner was dragged out, hoarsely begging for mercy.

Held by the feet, his body bouncing and scraping along the roadway, Ratliff was hauled to a vacant lot behind a movie theatre—where some 2000 frenzied men, women and children had gathered. "How d'you plead now, Santa— guilty or not guilty?" someone shouted, and the mob howled with glee. "We got a present for you, Santa!" an hysterical old woman cried, kicking up her legs in a ghastly war dance.

Undaunted hangmen

In this "trial" the verdict did not wait upon evidence. "Hang him, now!" came the shout and willing hands proffered a length of rope. One end of it was thrown up and over the top of a tall pole, supporting a power transformer, and the other clumsily fastened around Ratliff's neck in a makeshift hangman's noose. To the mob's cheers, eager volunteers hauled on the rope and, with a sudden jerk, Ratliff's body leapt into the air.

But it did not rise far. Suddenly, the rope snapped and Ratliff crashed to the ground. His hangmen were undaunted. A group hurried away and returned with a brand-new coil of hemp from a nearby hardware store. This was so stiff that no proper, running noose could be fashioned. A couple of men tied it around Ratliff's neck as best they could, and once more the "execution" was signalled.

Incoherent prayer

This time a long line of men formed on the downhaul end of the rope—some of them encouraging their small sons to join them and enjoy the thrill of the fatal pull. Ratliff lay on the ground, babbling what seemed to be an incoherent prayer. "D'you wanna say something, Santa?" a girl shrieked. "He's only talkin' religion," another answered.

"Heave!" a voice commanded, and the men and boys on the end of the rope marched smartly backwards. Legs wildly kicking, Ratliff's body rose into the night air.

Those at the very end of the line passed the rope's end around another pole and secured it. Then they and the rest of the grinning, cursing mob gathered beneath the swinging body and watched the kicking of the legs grow gradually feeble until it ceased altogether. Then a mighty shout filled the vacant lot. The "trial" was over.

rested content with the verdict, and brought no further charges against Hill.

So it seemed that the Santa Claus bank robbery trials were moving to their legal culmination. For Helms this was so, and in September 1929 he was carried, struggling furiously, to the electric chair.

But for Ratliff another trial looked imminent. He had persuaded his mother to secure a sanity hearing for him, and Judge Davenport ruled that he must be taken out of the penitentiary and back to Eastland County, where he had stood his first trial. He duly arrived there in October 1929, exhibiting all the signs of a man whose reason had departed. He walked like a zombie and appeared unable to feed or wash himself.

Ratliff was, in fact, making his final

SMART KID Woody Harris took the ignition-key when his parents' car was hi-jacked by the gang. Enterprising Woody grew up to be a local businessman.

attempt to cheat the law. He lulled the Eastland jailers into a false sense of security for a few days, lying inert and helpless on his bunk. Then one night he sprang to life, grasped a guard's gun and shot him. His hoped-for escape failed, but word quickly spread that Ratliff had killed the guard—although, in fact, a bullet had inflicted only a minor wound. Furious that Ratliff should be lying in a local cell and not in Death Row, a lynch mob came for him.

Now Marshall Ratliff faced a "trial" of such brutality as he had never envis-

'WE SHALL MAKE A GOOD BONFIRE OF HIM'

THE MOB came for him on Palm Sunday. They knew where he would be—in the Dominican convent of San Marco. It was there, in the high pulpit under the great golden cross, that Friar Girolamo Savonarola had thundered so often against vice and corruption, and particularly against vice and corruption within the Church he loved and served. From that pulpit, too, thrust into civic leadership by the march of history, he had ruled the state of Florence. But now feeling was running against him.

There was still time to escape. That was the course his closest followers urged on him. He did not listen. Instead he went out to face the howls and jeers of the mob. The story of Savonarola, the pious but unruly friar of Florence, was nearly over. The men who had once hung on his words dragged him away, like a common criminal, to torture and to death.

Good and evil

It has been common in the past to see the conflict between Savonarola and Alexander VI, second of the Borgia popes, as a straightforward clash between good and evil. It was not as simple as that. Certainly, Alexander VI was far from the kind of pope one would find occupying the throne of St. Peter today.

His uncle, Pope Calixtus III (1455-58), had made him a cardinal when he was only 24. By the time he himself was elected pontiff in 1492, he had enjoyed the pleasures of several mistresses and had fathered a number of illegitimate children, including the legendary Cesare and Lucrezia Borgia.

But this scandalous behaviour has to be seen against the background of the age in which it occurred. At the time, the Church was virtually the only profession open to clever and ambitious men. Furthermore, the Pope was not merely a spiritual ruler. The Church had vast temporal power and its leader was expected to be very much a man of the world, able to deal with princes and politicians as well as run the Church.

Simple faith

In the circumstances, high office, and even the position of pope itself, sometimes fell to men of little piety. But this was anathema to Savonarola. He sought a return to an earlier era of simple faith, when the Church was less concerned with wealth and elaborate ritual and in patronizing the work of great artists and sculptors. Above all, he wanted to see the affairs of the Church in the hands of men who kept God's commandments. He believed that he had a divine mission to bring this about.

Savonarola, with his great hooked nose, preached direct, emotional sermons, delivered with the zeal of a prophet. "Zeal,"

he said on one occasion, "is naught else than an intense love in the heart of the just man, which does not let him rest but ever seeks to remove all that he sees to be against the honour of God, whom he vehemently loves." He bade men constantly to turn for happiness and salvation to "the simplicity and the life of Christ and the true Christians". His attacks on Rome were often violent.

"You have become a shameless harlot in your lusts!" he cried in one sermon. "Oh, prostitute Church, you have displayed your foulness to the whole world, and you stink to high heaven."

Actually, the Pope, motivated perhaps by an uneasy conscience, appeared for a long time to take a fairly tolerant view of these outbursts. In the end, however, Savonarola overreached himself when he added hostile deeds to his hostile words.

LUCREZIA BORGIA was fathered by Pope Alexander VI (above) second of the Borgia pontiffs. His uncle, Pope Calixtus III (below) started the line.

Both Mansell

He plotted to have Alexander deposed. It was a fatal error. The personal life of Alexander might fall below the standards expected of the heir of St. Peter, but he was still the Pope and strongly conscious of the status of the Holy See. Savonarola paid for his misjudgement with his life.

Who was this man, driven by sanctity to try to overthrow the most powerful figure in Christendom?

Girolamo Savonarola, third of seven children, was born at Ferrara in Italy on September 21, 1452. Originally, he intended to become a doctor. The corruption of Renaissance society troubled him increasingly, however. "I cannot suffer the blind wickedness of the peoples of Italy," he wrote to his father, and, at the age of 22, without warning to his parents, he entered the Dominican order.

Visions

In July 1491, he became prior of San Marco in Florence. For some years, a strong prophetical note had run through most of his sermons. He claimed to have had visions from God. In addition to his attacks on vice, he claimed that the Church — and Italy — would suffer disaster. Only abandonment of the pursuit of pleasure and beauty could save them from the wrath of Heaven.

It was not exactly a popular message in a sophisticated city like Florence. Gradually, however, the undersized monk with the impassioned eyes, gleaming beneath his black cowl, began to make himself heard. His reputation spread. People flocked from all over Italy to hear him preach. Among them was the Renaissance painter, Sandro Botticelli, who went away inspired to paint his masterpieces of the nativity, "Adoration of the Shepherds", and of the Crucifixion.

Guidance and leadership

The congregations spilled out of the front door, down the steps, and across the square. There was never enough room for all those who wanted to hear him. Young men who had been drawn to his church in the first place out of idle curiosity suddenly found themselves with a vocation to serve God, and joined the Dominican order.

In 1494 it looked as if the friar's prediction that the Church and Italy would suffer a major disaster was about to come true. King Charles VIII of France, bent on a war of attrition, appeared with an army of 30,000 men at the gates of Florence. Piero de' Medici, ruler of the city, fled. In its moment of crisis, Florence turned to Savonarola for guidance

PIERO DE MEDICI (top), ruler of Florence, and Maximilian I, Holy Roman Emperor (far right), opposed Charles VIII, ambitious ruler of France.

and leadership.

The result was that the friar became the virtual dictator of Florence. His word was law. He came to an amicable settlement with Charles. He also set about righting all the "wrongs" of the Medici regime. In Florence he would create the City of God on earth which St. Augustine had dreamt of. It would be an example to Italy, to the world.

He was not motivated at any time by arrogance or self-seeking. An ambassador to Florence at the time reported: "He aims at nothing save the good of all, seeking for union and peace." Nevertheless, his statesmanship was betrayed by the hatred of vice against which he had so often thundered in the pulpit. His remarkable Christian commonwealth was, in many ways, wise and democratic. But there was also a fundamental intolerance springing from strong asceticism.

A great bonfire was lit – the Bonfire of the Vanities – in the Piazza della Signoria. Books, statues, paintings, musical instruments, carnival masks, and costumes were burned to ashes while the church bells of Florence rang out and Florentines danced around the fire, singing hymns.

Children were recruited, rather as the Nazis would recruit them four centuries

THE BONFIRE OF THE VANITIES – lit by order of Savonarola in the Piazza della Signoria, Florence. Hymns were sung as works of art were burned.

later. Savonarola's youngsters collected money for the poor, but it was also part of their duties to spy on their parents.

There can be no doubt that the friar, turned into a statesman by events, tried to do what he thought was right by God and the citizens of Florence. His efforts, however, brought him into conflict with the Pope in a far more direct way than had any of his strictures in the pulpit about the lax morals of Rome.

A political nuisance

It was only a century since the Church had been torn by schism with one pope ruling in Rome and another in Avignon. In face of the ambitions of Charles VIII, Alexander had formed a Holy Alliance. By 1495 it included Milan, Naples, Venice, Spain, and the Holy Roman emperor Maximilian I. Savonarola, however, remained on terms of friendship with the French king. He was also increasingly busy running his City of God which, he had come to believe, depended on his personal presence and inspiration if it was going to function.

It was inevitable that Alexander should see him as a political nuisance. The Pope fired the opening shot on July 21, 1495. It took the form of a courteous invitation for Savonarola to visit Rome and explain the revelations he claimed to have received from God. The friar sent a letter nine days later declining to make the trip for several reasons – he was unwell, he

might be murdered on the road, he was needed in Florence.

"So," he explained, "it is not God's will that I leave just now." He would, however, send the Pope a copy of the book he had written on his revelations.

The dispute between Savonarola and the Pope escalated over the next couple of years. For his part, Alexander issued a brief condemning the friar's claim to divine inspiration and suspending him from preaching. He also removed Savonarola from the post of Vicar-General of the Tuscan congregation of the Dominicans – to be reorganized as part of a new Roman-Lombardy congregation.

Initially, Savonarola responded by sending the Pope a five-point letter in which he pleaded his allegiance to the Holy See; denied that he had ever claimed to be an inspired prophet, but made the point that, if he had, it would not have implied unorthodoxy. He protested against the reorganization of the Dominican congregations, and objected to the appointment of the Vicar-General of the Lombardy congregation to head an inquiry into his visions.

Excommunicated

He followed that up by ignoring the reorganization of the congregations and continuing to rule over the Tuscan Dominicans as their Vicar-General. He also appeared intermittently in the pulpit, where his denunciations of the wickedness

of Rome grew more and more violent. Finally, on May 13, 1497, the Pope excommunicated him.

Savonarola immediately published a letter, addressed to "all Christians", in which he denied the validity of the excommunication. He did not, however, preach again that year, and, on October 13, asked for a pardon. The Pope did not reply. The friar, stung at being ignored, took the defiant step of saying Mass in public on Christmas Day. He started preaching again on February 11, making the challenging statement in his first sermon: "Anyone who accepts that my excommunication is valid is a heretic."

By this time Savonarola's earlier popularity had begun to wane. In the way of human affairs, there had been a swing away from the City of God towards the former City of Mammon. The friar's political opponents grew daily more powerful. There were also fears that, if Florence supported Savonarola too openly and enthusiastically, the Pope might retaliate by placing an edict of punishment on the whole city.

It was at this point that the friar took his fatal step. He claimed that Alexander was not a valid pope because he had bought the votes which elected him to office. He repeated the charge in letters he sent to the kings of England (Henry VII), France, Hungary, Italy, Spain, and Emperor Maximilian, and he invited them to a Council to depose the Pope.

Ordeal by fire

It was a situation in which the Pope had no choice but to take strong and positive action. Before he could move, however, matters were taken out of his hands. In Florence, a Franciscan monk had challenged Savonarola to an ordeal by fire to prove the truth of his claims. Savonarola rejected the offer, but it was taken up by a follower, Domenico da Pescia.

In the event the ordeal did not take place. Not only did it rain heavily; the Franciscan failed to turn up. The frustration and disappointment of the large crowd that had gathered in the Piazza della Signoria in the hope of witnessing a sign from Heaven, plus the unease caused by Savonarola's long dispute with the Pope, sparked off a popular reaction against the friar. So, on Palm Sunday, he and Domenico da Pescia and a second follower, Silvestro Maruffi, were seized by the mob.

The Pope demanded that the three monks should be sent to Rome. Savonarola's enemies—and there were by now many of them—in Florence insisted that he should be tried "in the city where he committed his crimes". It is usually said that Savonarola had to face the ordeal of three trials, two by his civil accusers, one by the Church. Use of the word "trial" can be misleading.

In a case like Savonarola's, a Renaissance trial was more like a political trial in the old Soviet Union than the processes of justice common in the Western world. The guilt of the prisoner and the death sentence were assumed. The only purpose of the trial was to persuade him, by torture if necessary, to confess the error of his ways.

The *strappado*

The method of torture used on Savonarola was called the *strappado*. It was not the worst available, but it was agony while it lasted and left permanent injuries. It consisted of hanging a prisoner by the hands with a rope over a pulley. He was hauled up, dropped, then stopped with a jerk.

The degree of suffering could be easily controlled by the speed of the drop and the severity of the jerk which ended it. The *strappado* dislocated shoulders, broke arms, tore muscles, and maimed hands. In cases of extreme stubbornness, prisoners were allowed to drop right to the floor, crippling them for life.

The *strappado* was used on Savonarola for days on end. One witness said he saw him dropped right to the floor no fewer than 14 times in the course of one evening. His torturers carefully suspended him by only one arm, the left, leaving the right hand free to sign a confession.

Although his two followers withstood the agony, Savonarola—highly-strung and sensitive—finally capitulated and confessed to his "crimes". As soon as the torture ceased, however, he withdrew his confession. He was brought back for a second trial on the *strappado*. Then, after he had once again confessed under

SAVONAROLA was tortured by *strappado* (left). This was an agonizing form of torture which could leave a prisoner crippled for life.

pain that "he had not received from God the things he preached", the final stage of his ordeal began.

The Pope sent two commissioners to Florence to examine him. One was a Judge Romolino. "We shall make a good bonfire of him," said Romolino uncompromisingly on his arrival. The examination began in May 1498, with Savonarola already maimed and exhausted.

The main concern of the commissioners was the friar's attempt to call a Council of European rulers to depose the Pope on the grounds that he had bought the votes that put him on the chair of St. Peter. Was it not true that he had said that Alexander, who had Moorish blood, had not been baptized, and was therefore not even a Christian? Was it not true also

that Savonarola had failed to conform to his excommunication?

"I confess having done evil and that I am a sinner," said the friar. "But I ask for mercy."

Romolino, dissatisfied with his answer, ordered the monk to be made ready for the *strappado* again. Terrified, Savonarola threw himself on his knees before the commissioners and pleaded: "God, hear me. You have me caught. I confess I have denied Christ and I have lied."

However, he then turned to Florentine nobles present in the court and, with tears running down his face and his twisted left arm held out to them, recanted, saying: "Be my witness of this. I have told lies because of my fear of the torture. If I must suffer, let me suffer for

the truth. I said what I said because I received it from God."

So they tortured him again for two more days. It was much the same as in the previous two trials. In his agony, Savonarola would confess to anything. Then, when he was released from the *strappado* and the pain had subsided, he withdrew the confession. "Oh, help me, Jesus," he pleaded between his groans. "Do not tear my body. I will tell you the truth, the certain truth."

Yes, he had preached a new form of

AFTER ADMITTING his faults, Savonarola (left inset) and his two companions were hanged (left) and then burnt. Below, the "heretic's" austere study preserved today as it was in his time.

BOTTICELLI heard Savonarola preach and painted his portrait (above). The great painter's "Crucifixion" (left) was inspired by the sermon.

Christianity. No, he had had no fear of censure or excommunication. Yes, it had been an act of pride, folly, and blindness to plot against the Pope. No, he had given no thought to the great scandal which would result from his attempts to call a Council to depose Alexander.

Yet, as soon as he was taken down from the *strappado,* he withdrew all these admissions. Why? "The torture does not make me tell the truth," he groaned to the commissioners. "I fear it so much it makes me confess to anything." By the end of the second day, the commissioners accepted that there was no point in continuing with their inquisition. Savon-

arola would merely go on alternately confessing and recanting

On May 22 he and his two followers were taken out to the Piazza della Signoria and publicly hanged. A huge fire was then lit beneath the suspended bodies.

A saint?

But that was not to be the end of the story of the man who tried to create a City of God on earth, and reform the Church he loved. Before his ashes were cold, men who still felt the call of his piety and sincerity raked among them for mementos. Within a year, there was talk in Florence of miracles — one of the

signs of a saint — worked by Savonarola.

He has continued to haunt the centuries. He has been revered by men of sanctity like Philip Neri, himself canonized by the Roman Catholic Church. One of the friar's biographers wrote: "No one will be found to deny the essential goodness and purity of his vision in those dark days for the Church."

As late as 1952, the 500th anniversary of Savonarola's birth, there were calls for him to be declared a saint. That honour may yet be accorded to the "intolerant friar of Florence" of whom it has been said: "Had his voice been listened to, perhaps, beyond the Alps, Luther would not have arisen."